India in Transition

India in Transition
Essays from a Nation Remade

Prafull Goradia

Published by
Renu Kaul Verma
Vitasta Publishing Pvt Ltd
4348/4C, Ansari Road, Daryaganj
New Delhi-110 002
info@vitastapublishing.com

ISBN: 978-93-47098-92-5

First Edition 2026
MRP ₹ 495

Typeset by Shubhpreet Kaur
Cover Design by Rohit Gautam
Printed by Vikas Computer and Printers, New Delhi

Contents

International Politics

Economics

Cultural

Preface

The declared purpose of any compendium that gathers articles written across the shifting seasons of a nation's political, economic, social, and cultural life is never to proclaim, with misplaced grandeur, that it contains the full and final history of that nation. Such a claim would be not only extravagant but fundamentally untrue, for no single volume—however ambitious, however meticulously curated—can hope to clasp the entirety of a civilisation's lived experience between its covers. And yet, despite the modesty of its intentions, every such compilation inevitably becomes a mirror, catching fragments of the past and refracting them into the present. History, like a patient visitor, finds its way into the margins, whispers through commentary, and lingers in the patterns that emerge across disparate essays. The very attempt to examine the present makes the shadow of the past impossible to ignore.

In India's case, this reflective quality is even more pronounced. Few will contest that India has undergone a metamorphosis so profound that it often appears unrecognisable from the country it was merely a decade ago. Its transformation is not a single event but an ongoing chronicle—a tale that has only just begun to unfold, even as its early chapters astonish observers with the speed and scale of change. To capture this evolution is to watch a tapestry alter its colours while it is still on the loom.

The political watershed of 2014 stands as one of the defining hinges of this narrative. The shift in the ruling establishment was not merely electoral; it was atmospheric, almost tectonic. It rearranged expectations, destabilised older certainties, and injected a new vocabulary into public life. To catalogue the consequences of that moment would require a tome of formidable proportions—a work chronicling how institutions were reimagined, how governance was reconceived, and how national priorities were reordered with striking confidence. The change was not quiet; it was clarifying. It announced itself through decisive gestures, ambitious schemes, and a redefinition of the nation's self-image.

Once dismissed as part of the "Fragile Five," India has since ascended to become the world's fourth-largest economy—a feat that speaks not only to economic policy but to a shift in collective temperament. A nation once wary of speaking too loudly of its own aspirations, often apologetic about the scale of its ambitions, has begun to articulate its interests on the world stage with a newfound steadiness. This change is discernible not only in geopolitical posturing or diplomatic rhetoric but also in the country's cultural pulse: a more confident, less diffident understanding of its own civilisational memory and contemporary potential.

Yet the story is far more intricate than a simple tale of rise and revival. Politics continues to twist and ripple like a monsoon river, cutting unexpected channels, challenging settled analyses, and producing undercurrents that elude easy prediction.

Electoral landscapes shift, alliances fracture and reform, and the democratic imagination repeatedly reinvents itself. To watch Indian politics is to witness a living organism that refuses stasis.

Equally compelling—though quieter in their unfolding—are the social transformations underway. These are not always measured in headlines or hashtags. They take root in altered social interactions, in the subtle redefinition of identities, in the ways families, communities, and individuals grapple with modernity, aspiration, and tradition. The digital revolution, reaching even the furthest corners of the country, has democratised information and aspirations alike. New forms of mobility—economic, geographic, and social—have begun to reorder long-standing hierarchies. A country that once moved at a cautious pace now seems propelled by an impatience that borders on restlessness: a desire to break through constraints, to claim opportunity, to be counted.

It is within this dynamic, restless, evolving India that this volume finds its purpose. It does not pretend to provide a definitive account of the nation's journey, nor does it seek to offer a comprehensive historical verdict. Instead, it gathers moments, perspectives, fragments—a mosaic assembled from the vantage points of different times and contexts. It is an attempt to observe the unfolding drama with clarity, to trace the outlines of change as they appear on the national canvas, and to contribute, however modestly, to the continuing conversation about who we were, who we are, and who we might yet become.

If this volume succeeds at all, it is only in lending a shoulder—small but earnest—to the grand endeavour of understanding India's ongoing transformation.

National Politics

Olympic Torch Boycotted While Passing through Srinagar

Pakistani rulers suffer from a number of obsessions; the Olympic torch passing through Srinagar before eventually reaching Chennai is one of many. How unfortunate that so many of their aspiring chess players were denied the opportunity to play on this world platform at the recent Olympiad at Chennai. This was a fleeting whim but now to trade with India is a chromic denial of so many needed items. Why? Presumably, to teach India a lesson. Just because India and Pakistan were born simultaneously, in August 1947, Islamabad has taken it for granted that the two countries are comparable if not equal. How presumptuous to believe that a country and its rulers are, more or less, equal to a neighbour seven times larger! What is more remarkable is that India, at least until 2014 when the BJP came to power, also played along with the Pakistani mania of comparability, if not equality. The damage done to India's image over the years was far greater.

The expert on *Strategy*: Edward Luttwak years ago innovated the concept of Armed Suasion which, if pursued, would make one's country appear stronger than it really was. His favourite example was pre-World War II Italy which was then widely believed to be the most powerful air power in Europe. Foreign affairs become easier to conduct with Armed Suasion than without it. The most recent example was that of China which appeared too powerful to be challenged in Taiwan. But when Nancy Pelosi, the Speaker of the U S House of Representatives decided to visit Taipei, against Chinese wishes, and did visit, the Chinese government could not do anything to prevent her. But until her aeroplane landed at Taipei and she attended the required official functions in the city and flew out, there was tension. India, as designated by the Nehru government, was the opposite. India and Pakistan were bracketed together.

When war came, in 1947, 1965 and 1971 with Pakistan, the question on most lips was: who would win? Why should there have been any question? For a Pakistan chess team to indicate to the world in Chennai that Islamabad does not still accept that Kashmir is an integral part of India is a show of defiance. It is the result of seventy-four years of inaction or weak action. To offer only one blunder of inaction as an example was the Simla Conference of 1972 between Indira Gandhi and Zulfikar Bhutto following the 1971 war. It was settled between the two leaders that the Line of Control (Loc), that divides Kashmir and its part that Pakistan had gobbled up in 1947/48, would be the international border. There was to be no dispute on Kashmir after India returned the 93,000 prisoners of war taken in Bangladesh the previous year. We promptly returned the prisoners but let the LoC be until Bhutto could consolidate his position in his country. He had become Prime Minister only after the 1971 war ended. If this is how we run foreign affairs, instead of Armed Suasion, India would be known for its Disarmed Suasion and be pushed about by any of its neighbours and adversaries; not to say that the current government in Delhi is pursing such a weak-kneed policy. To this day not a single POW has remained in India. The LoC is as it was.

How our government mishandled the China policy from the beginning until 1962 is well known, but there was a way out even after all the mishandling. Our officers knew in the first few days that the Indian forces was not prepared or equipped to be able to cope with either the enemy or the terrain or the weather which was freezing cold. Moreover, any additional troops that the Army could send up to the mountains were going to be wearing their flimsy woollen pullovers, thin socks, no gloves and many of the soldiers had no better than canvas shoes. How on earth could such ill-equipped troops fight? Any enemy who wished to conquer and keep territory would normally launch an attack in spring and not autumn. The Chinese invasion commenced on 20 October 1962. The opportunity for India was to withdraw to the plains of Assam where the terrain, the weather and the clothes, would be congenial. The Chinese would have had to occupy the Arunachal or NEFA then hillside through the bitter cold. Meanwhile, our Army would have gained time and been better equipped for a spring battle on conditions more of our choosing. But we did not do any of this and our soldiers suffered.

As it turned out, the Chinese wanted to teach the Indian government a lesson and display their military superiority, which they did. They declared a unilateral withdrawal on 21 November 1962. Their troops returned home with their prestige flying high.

Decline in Congress

It is inaccurate to say that it is Rahul Gandhi who has precipitated the decline of the Congress party. The seeds of the downward journey were sown in the years after Indira Gandhi separated and formed the Congress (Ruling) in 1969. The seeds became visible after her landslide victory in the *Garibi Hatao* poll in 1972. In the euphoric mood of triumph, a coterie grew around her. R K Dhawan and Makhanlal Fotedar became the two trusted custodians, especially for dealing with visitors, the Congressmen. Gradually, with the progress of time and the growth of power, they became conduits for initiating contact with any of the partymen. As time went on, most chief ministers thought it was essential to have a close link with one of the two custodians, preferably the former. After all, how much work could Mrs Gandhi attend to personally? The late Madhavsinh Solanki, the then CM of Gujarat happened to mention in my presence that he preferred making courtesy calls on the PM in Delhi. For the more serious work, it was best to communicate through Dhawan. For advice, when needed, Finance Minister Pranab Mukherjee was excellent. Arjun Singh, the CM of Madhya Pradesh, operated through Fotedar.

A few senior Congressmen, when they met privately, would express their resentment against having to deal with officers and stenographers rather than the political leaders.

In my Kolkata days, I quite often went to see Ajit Panja, who eventually became the Information and Broadcasting Minister at the Centre, I met him when he was the president of the West Bengal Pradesh Congress Committee. The party had no office; I, therefore, had to go to his house. Once when I was with him, a senior Congress member called Mohammad Ali came to see him. He and Panja chatted for a few minutes. Ali soon got up to go and while leaving told his host, 'This is the last time you are seeing me at home. I can go to any *masjid* or *mandir* to meet a *maulvi* or *pujari*, but not to their homes. Similarly, I can visit a politician only in his office'.

When he had departed, Panja turned to me and asked, "Where can I get a political office, when New Delhi doesn't sanction any money for rent?" West Bengal had hardly any District Congress Committee functioning. In fact, many of the DCC presidents chose the Congress in order to retain the offices. Later, at Delhi I was told that half the DCCs of the Indira Congress did not exist. My informant went on to say that Mrs Gandhi was not in favour of assets and property. She might have believed that such assets do not attract power, but can lure politicians. So, why have them in the first place? The other lesson she had learnt was that satraps should be shunned by the top leadership; that was her 1969 experience when the original Congress split into two. If the top leader had the mass following that would be the secret of success. The satraps could in troubled times compete with the top.

The key to success in Indira Gandhi's scheme of things was that the top leader had to have charismatic appeal. The party then has no choice but to follow the leader. In this grand strategy, if the charisma slips, the entire party slips even more.

The reason is that the second line of leadership sees this as its chance to get on top. To that extent, Indira Gandhi left a difficult legacy. Only a rare individual could be so charismatic. Yet, surprisingly, Rajiv Gandhi rose to the occasion riding on the assassination of his mother as well as his own attractiveness. As we know, the Congress led by him won over 400 seats in the 1984 Lok Sabha election. He made a flying start but unfortunately, he never understood politics as he did machines, whether aircraft or gadgets.

When Rajiv came to power he did not realise how to connect with the Indian masses, something his mother could instinctively do. Even then, he could have managed as Indira's offspring, but he dressed unusually well, wore Italian Gucci shoes and American Ray Ban sunglasses; he even said in a magazine interview that he liked pork sandwiches. All these things belonged to a highly Westernised wealthy elite. The Congress began to get alienated from the poor Indians; it began ceasing to be "our party" for many voters.

After Rajiv was assassinated and Narasimha Rao completed his Prime Ministership, the following two general elections were not Congress victories, as much as the BJP's defeats, which had abandoned its traditional ideology and could not field leaders who could win votes. In the bargain, the Congress was able to form a coalition for two consecutive terms. It got 144 seats in 2004 and yet managed to cobble together a coalition at the Centre.

All that has been written above in a way explains how the Congress' decline began with the end of Indira Gandhi. Rahul Gandhi alone cannot be blamed for the slow decay the party has suffered.

Democracy

Traversing the last several months, one would be hard pressed to read a newspaper or remember a television channel wherein someone has not complained that in India, democracy is being bypassed, or that "democracy is in danger". Or, the more politically fashionable accusation that we are being ruled by "fascist forces" who are hell bent on devouring democracy. Suffice it to say of such accusers that they do not have any idea of what fascism is, leave alone the historical circumstances that birthed this ideology.

If one were, for the sake of argument, to entertain the accusation that democracy is indeed in danger, the natural corollary to such an accusation would be: from whence does this "danger to democracy" arise? If democracy is supposedly imperiled because of the ruling dispensation, why then do not the Opposition parties gather to unite and try to win elections whenever and wherever they are held? The meetings and conclaves for forming *Mahagathbandhans* have been many but seldom does a *bandhan* emerge.

In years past, I have sat in Parliament and participated in

its proceedings actively. During the time I was a member, not once did we walk out. Nor did the Congress Opposition walk out. There were a significant number of Marxists too. What I clearly learnt is that, for the opposition, Parliament is the best platform to perform on. Its two main faces are: to oppose by pointing out the flaws in policies of the government and equally to seize opportunities to project their programmes when they come to power.

For the last many Parliament sessions, I cannot remember any of the Opposition members projecting what policies they propose to follow when they came to power. What an exquisite opportunity it is for the Opposition to propagate its manifesto on the floor of the Parliament with the TV channels blazing. But lately, and especially since 2004, it has been a frequent occurrence for the Opposition members to rush to the well of the house and force an adjournment.

The session time lost is mostly a loss for the Opposition, which has few other televised platforms to articulate on a national scale. For the government, so long as it can have its legislation passed, its task is accomplished. But what does the Opposition gain? Quite a large segment of the people watching the spectacle of walkouts feel that the MPs draw their salaries and benefits but do very little or no work.

There are more effective ways of protesting, such as wearing black, sitting on the staircase and not their seats. To tell the public watching television, they could carry a few posters. The Opposition parties can think of other peaceable ways whereby the public can know of the protest, yet the Houses of Parliament can carry on. Democracy even then would seem to be alive and kicking. The legislatures would seem to be working and the executive would appear to be taken to task from time to time.

Anything done to obstruct the public institutions from working would eventually hurt the interests of the minorities, the Opposition and any group with fewer members. It is remarkable how well democracy has dug deep roots in our country despite all its diversities, including many people lagging behind in education. Dynasties have successfully cropped up over the decades because leaders have preferred to give short shrift to ideologies, programmes and manifestos. As it is, in a country of diversities and different languages, communication is difficult which is why voters find it easier to identify with personalities rather than programmes.

The lasting link between the voter and ruler is the trust that the former develops in the latter. The election of a candidate is a choice of the voter between the candidates who contest in his/her constituency. By and large, there is common sense behind the choice. I go back to 1962 after the Chinese invasion. Logically, the then ruling party, i.e., the Congress, should have been wiped out. But this did not happen. What was the quality of the opposing candidates across the country? And were they organised enough to be relied upon to govern the country? How is the situation any better today? To the thinking citizen, floor crossing in hordes or large groups, with the now all-too-common drama of legislators being bundled off and held captive in five-star hotels, supposedly to prevent their poaching by other parties, is not funny at all. There are a number of faults that contribute to reducing the voter's trust in the system. After all, the very people who routinely express fears about democracy and its future are the people who readily cross the assembly floor.

Pakistan Coming Apart

In my book, *Jinnah Helped Hindus*, written a couple of years ago, I had argued that Indians would have been distinctly worse off had Jinnah not sought and attained the Partition of India. Without the vivisection, an undivided India would have included the two Pakistans (to our east and west). Today's Bangladesh would also have been our citizens. Their Prime Minister Sheikh Hasina visited New Delhi and went back with a loan of 9.5 billion dollars. To be honest, as recently as 1991, India too had to borrow from wherever it could, including pawning its own gold. It is only the balance of payments crisis of that year that forced us to end our toxic romance with socialism.

But of overriding importance for India now is the steadily deteriorating scenario next door. Many journalists as well as other participants debating on Pakistani television have lately been expressing their anxiety about whether their country will remain intact. Over the years, we Indians disregarded the likelihood of further breakup of that country (Pakistan first broke apart in the 1971 war, with the secession of its erstwhile East Pakistan which became Bangladesh), as its population overwhelmingly belongs to one religion. Muslims in India who had contacts in the neighbouring country, after the first flush of Partition, did not emigrate to Pakistan. We were misled by the spectacle of Pak cricketers being applauded. Those who really understood Pakistan had no interest in migrating. They knew that the neighbouring country did not have a nationality. It is nationality that constitutes a national soul which moves by a single spiritual principle.

The soul is a result of a rich heritage of memories and is the outcome of a past of common efforts, sacrifices and devotion. The principle evolves out of a heroic glory. This is a form of social capital upon which a national idea is built and endures. The distinguished French philosopher and scholar Ernest Renan has written extensively on this in his book *What is a Nation*?

Evidently, East Pakistan had nothing in common with West Pakistan except religion. Punjab and Sind are neighbours, but what is common between them? Little wonder that G M Saeed, the Sindhi leader, initiated a separatist movement called *Jio Sind* decades ago. What is common between the Pathan and the Punjabi? The former's memory is linked to Afghanistan whereas the latter's upper class chooses to look upon Arab and Central Asian medieval invaders as its ancestors. Most Balochs are Shias, whom the Sunni Punjabis are trying to expel from Islam.

There was no question of any migration or separation until they were rulers. It was only with the advent of the twentieth century that thirty-five Muslim eminences led by the Aga Khan went to call on Viceroy Lord Minto at Simla, to press for special privileges for Muslims, like separate electorates and reservations in government jobs. Five months later, the Muslim League was founded at Dacca (now Dhaka). The League's office-bearers were largely from United Provinces (UP).

The movement for a separate state for the Muslims of the subcontinent was driven primarily by the Muslims inhabiting Uttar Pradesh and Bihar, today called Mohajirs, and the rich Muslim merchants from Bombay, who feared they would be beaten in any trade and industrial competition with the Hindus in an undivided India after the British left. This is not to say that the idea of Pakistan had no sympathy whatsoever from Muslims in other parts of India. Indeed, Muslims in the former Madras state and Travancore were supportive. The 1946 elections, in which close to 96 per cent of the Muslim electorate cast its vote in favour of Partition, is sufficient to substantiate this point.

The irony, however, is that the provinces that eventually became Pakistan had no enthusiasm for Jinnah's project of a separate Muslim homeland for India's Muslims. Bengal was not regarded as 'truly' Muslim by either the ulema or ummah. In fact, it was the barely disguised northwestern Muslims' contempt for Bengalis that was a major factor in its separation from Pakistan in 1971. The Pathans of the northwest, closely aligned with Afghanistan, have never recognised the state of Pakistan. Punjab, an agrarian state, distrusted Jinnah, while Sind, whose people are given to business and commerce, were forced to separate from India. Balochistan was anyway a separate kingdom. Yet, Qwaid-e-Azam Jinnah did achieve his quest of a separate Pakistan.

Although Pakistan has been a state since 1947, it is not a nation and will never be. As things stand, we can see it unfastening, with its heads of state and government begging virtually every country for continual monetary aid. In the lack of nationhood lies the genesis of Pakistan—religious hatred of Hindus, but nothing else. Pakistan's debilitating irony is exacerbated by the fact that the basis on which it claims to have been founded, i.e., Islam, stoutly disavows the idea of a nation, whereas, in the modern world of the civilisational nation-state, no state can survive without nationhood. Little wonder that Pakistan is coming apart.

On Divide and Rule

"Divide and rule" would be a ready excuse for many an Indian to use where he/she cannot explain the cause of say, a Hindu-Muslim riot, or any other such dispute or conflict. Tactically, an official or a local politician using this excuse is understandable, but for a person who knows modern Indian history, routinely dishing out this excuse is unpardonable.

The East India Company began its political career in present-day Madras or Chennai, a settlement which they founded. Its core officers and soldiers lived in their fort. The first Governor was Andrew Cogan. The Company's business activities then spread to Bombay, which had been given by the King of Portugal to his son-in-law, England's King Charles II, who gave the islands to the Company as a gift on lease of £10 per annum. The first Governor of the city was Gerald Aungier, who developed the fishing village into a township and established its headquarters at Fort George (not St George, which was the East India Company's name for its Madras settlement). All this happened in the late 1660s.

The East India Company's first commercial establishment

was opened in 1644, although it was developed into a full-fledged settlement with the building of Fort William and the acquisition of Govindpur, Kolkata and Sutanoti from the nawab of Bengal. However, the founding of Calcutta city by the legendary Job Charnock is dated to 1690. But the city had to wait until 1700 for its first Governor, when Sir Charles Eyre was installed. The three establishments were known as Presidencies, quite independent from one another; they directly reported to the Company's London headquarters.

There was no postal service in India in those days although ships came and went from these three ports. There was no particular complaint with regard to this arrangement. Nevertheless, the Westminster parliament—not the East India Company's Court of Directors—chose to pass the Regulating Act of 1773, whereby the Governors of Bombay and Madras were asked to begin reporting to Fort William at Calcutta. The Governor at Calcutta then was designated the Governor-General in India. This was evidence enough that the English government did not have "divide and rule" in its mind. Had it been otherwise, London would have allowed the three Presidencies to grow independent of one another and flower as three separate countries, and not bunch them together as one administrative entity.

One must assume that it was difficult for people in London in the seventeenth and eighteenth centuries to appreciate the significance of communal rivalry prevalent in India. But then how would several other measures, encouraging rather than discouraging steps that would ultimately lead to an integrating India, be explained?

The Indian Civil Services (ICS), which later birthed the Indian Administrative Service (IAS) that runs independent

India's administration and other senior services need not have been all-India institutions; they could have been different in the different Presidencies. For instance, the civil administrative services in Sri Lanka (then Ceylon) and Burma were distinct and did not have similarity with India.

If Macaulay's formula of introducing English education in the country had not been proposed and then implemented, an Oriya might have found it difficult to communicate with his Bihari neighbour. What if the English rulers had chosen to structure the armed forces Presidency-wise, rather than under a single umbrella?

A common currency is a boon but having to change one's currency notes when crossing over from one Presidency to another certainly isn't. Had such a measure not been implemented by the British, would the free flow of trade and commerce in the entire country have even been conceivable? Just imagine what the level of India's contact is with Pakistan on one hand and Bangladesh on another. Myanmar, then called Burma, was a province of British India until 1937. What is our level of understanding and interaction with that country today, even though it is our next-door neighbour?

Mohammed Ali Jinnah, who founded Pakistan, was candid enough to say that Pakistan was born the day the first Hindu was converted. That happened early in the eighth century AD. Since then, India was invaded continually until 1760 AD. Only during the fifty-year reign of Emperor Akbar and his successors Emperors Jahangir and Shah Jahan was there cordiality between communities. Otherwise, most of the time, there was at least an undercurrent of discord, especially due to the imposition of *jaziya* on the one hand and temple desecration on the other; both measures were the hallmark of the rule of Aurangzeb. By the end of his reign, the Rajputs, Sikhs, Jats and finally the Marathas were in open revolt. Aurangzeb admitted his failure in his letters to his sons saying, "I come and go as a stranger. I know not who I am. I lacked in leadership and in my duty in protecting the people". Aurangzeb also expressed the fear that his officials and troops would be ill-treated (by his enemies) after his death.

All this made sure that the two communities could not see eye to eye again. Even the Partition could not fully heal the wounds. Why, therefore, the insistence of laying blame only upon the British for "divide and rule?"

Nehru's Blunders

Minister Kiren Rijiju did well to bring into public focus Jawaharlal Nehru's mistakes in Kashmir as well as his handling of China policy. The blunders have cost India incalculably in blood, money and prestige. Nehru had three gurus, namely, his father Motilal, Gandhi and Krishna Menon. Motilal would have pointed out to his son that a quarter of India's population was Muslim and in an undivided sub-continent could be well over 40 per cent. Until May 1947, it was not certain that there would be a Partition. Jawaharlal was, therefore, modelled to lead Muslims; the Hindus were bound to fall in line behind a Brahmin willy-nilly. So much so, that even his wedding invitation card was printed in Urdu. This model came useful even after Partition for Nehru needed Muslims as the larger chunk of his vote bank. One has to recall that Sardar Vallabhbhai Patel was the Congress party's unanimously elected choice to be its president and then Prime Minister.

In any case, Gandhi was the Congress' role model for being pro-Muslim to the hilt. He even went to the extent of becoming President of the Khilafat Committee soon after World War I when the new reformist and revolutionary Turkish leader Kemal Mustafa, as well as the victorious British, dethroned and exiled the Caliph of all Sunni Islam and also the Sultan of the defeated Ottoman Empire. India had nothing to do with Turkey; indeed, Mohammed Ali Jinnah, then a prominent Congress leader (the day of his championing the Muslim separatist cause was still years away)kept away from the Khilafat Movement. But Gandhi would not be dissuaded from championing the cause of Islamic obscurantism.

Krishna Menon was the third in Nehru's trinity of gurus. He was a closet communist on whom Nehru leaned on for ideological guidance in defence and foreign affairs. It was he who convinced Nehru that China, a socialist country led by Mao Zedong, would not clash with India on the battlefield. At most, it could differ on policy issues. In any case, India should project itself as a socialist power. That would match with the country's stance of being anti-imperialist in the light of its history, and be in tune with its aspiration to lead the Third World. This advice was music to Nehru's ears. Little did Jawaharlal anticipate that in 1956, Britain and France would attack Colonel Nasser's Egypt, and only a few months later Khrushchev's Soviet Union would brutalise its satellite Hungary with tanks and guns. As a Third World leader and a personal friend of Nasser, India's Prime Minister condemned the Anglo-French invasion in the bitterest of words. But Nehru was nonplussed when Hungary was attacked. He had to say something critical and therefore said: "Violence seldom solves anything. We hope that the dark clouds over Budapest would clear before long".

Similarly, the Indian Prime Minister was so taken aback by the Chinese aggression in 1962 that he was driven to tears while speaking on All India Radio: "My heart goes out to the people of Assam," he said. Nehru's words conveyed the impression that Assam was lost.

Jawaharlal Nehru's blunders in Kashmir should be attributed to his friendship with Sheikh Abdullah; the latter was popularly called "Lion of the Valley". In actual fact, he was popular only among those who spoke the Kashmiri language. Once one crossed over to Muzaffarabad or Mirpur, where Punjabi is spoken, the Abdullah writ did not run. It was, therefore, the Sheikh's advice to Nehru to not include those areas in his planning. This according to the late Prof Balraj Madhok, an RSS member and politician from Jammu was the reason for India agreeing to a ceasefire, as it were, on the orders of the United Nations. That is how Pakistan-Occupied Kashmir (POK) was born. The responsibility for obeying the United Nations was attributed to the last Viceroy, Mountbatten.

Prof Balraj Madhok, who grew up in Iskardu where his father was in state service, consistently resented the fact that such personal likes and dislikes should influence national policies. Nevertheless, that was the beginning of the war of blood and money, which concluded with the abolition of Article 370. The idea of a separate flag and constitution for Kashmir was also Sheikh Abdullah's insistence. To facilitate their introduction, Article 370 was inserted as a Cabinet decision by Nehru. It never had the approval of India's Parliament. Sheikh Abdullah was such a favourite of Nehru that when he was released from Tihar Jail, he was driven straight to the Prime Minister's residence at Teen Murti, where he stayed until Nehru died. In contrast, Maharaja Hari Singh, who was disliked by the Sheikh, was dethroned and sent to Mumbai, although he remained a titular king of Kashmir.

Another of Nehru's weaknesses was a contradiction between

the animosity of Pakistanis, the 'Kashmiryat' of J & K, which had to be assuaged and the Indian Muslims who had to be kept happy for their votes. As a result, it was difficult to think clearly and Nehru certainly did not do so. In the process, India's national interests were dispatched to the backwaters of confusion.

The Congress's Woes

In 2022, the developments inside the Congress were enough to outdo the best of television soaps. The Gandhi dynasty, realising that it needed to present a face as its official president, put forth the octogenarian Mallikarjun Kharge as its preferred choice to act as a family retainer carrying the label of party president. The flamboyant and West-educated Shashi Tharoor, squashing talk of his having withdrawn from the race said that he is very much in what he called a "friendly contest", but nonetheless described it as a "fight to the finish". Congress veteran and former Madhya Pradesh Chief Minister Digvijay Singh was reported to have thrown his hat in the ring, only to withdraw. Diggy sahib inadvertently let the cat out of the bag when he told a journalist that whoever became the Congress president would have to work with the blessings of the Gandhi family. Translated, this reads: the Gandhi dynasty was, is and will remain the real boss, even if somebody else occasionally gets to sit on the chair.

Which is why Rajasthan Chief Minister Ashok Gehlot, whose loyalty to Sonia Gandhi was not in doubt and who was reportedly her choice to occupy the chair, had no qualms about letting her down. Gehlot's loyal MLAs kicked off a storm in the state unit of the party, threatening to bring down the government if the CM's rival Sachin Pilot was made the chief minister after Gehlot became Congress president. While the internal drama of the Congress may interest journalists and news-watchers, what must engage our attention is why India's oldest political party was so bereft of any leadership outside the Gandhi family, whose political cloud had dissipated to the extent that it no longer was taken seriously, leave alone command respect.

Political parties, whether in power or opposition, have a duty towards the country, and more so those parties that have a history like the Congress. As it appears, the Congress did not seem devoted to this idea. Its only calling card was blind hatred of Prime Minister Modi, which has no place in democracy. An opponent is an adversary, nothing more. Abuses like *chowkidar chor hai* only betray the speaker's character and pollute the political atmosphere.

The Congress has mostly functioned on the Führer Prinzip or the leadership principle. From 1921, Mohandas Gandhi continued to dominate the party until 1946. Then it was the turn of Jawaharlal Nehru, especially after Sardar Patel's passing away. He was followed by his illustrious daughter Indira Gandhi and in turn by her son Rajiv Gandhi, who knew or understood little of politics but managed somehow for five years. But he left a dent in the party. The poor men and women ceased to think it was their party. It was now the organisation of the rich who wore Gucci shoes, Ray-Ban glasses and so on.

However, the Congress was still not seen as an anti-Hindu outfit. After P V Narasimha Rao completed his term as Prime Minister, the party began to slide down that path. The 'consensus' that only a Nehru-Gandhi could hold the party together began to be spoken about more publicly. Thus, Sonia Gandhi was virtually fished out for the presidentship of the Congress. She did hold the party together for ten years, also enabling it to return to power, not by hit or miss but by mediocre partiality. The secret was Ahmed Patel, who was loyal to Indira Gandhi right through the Emergency. He was a young MP from Bharuch in Gujarat. While he was not, by any means, a rabid Muslim, he felt that the future of Muslims in India lay in moderation and the Congress. No other party was dependable and capable of keeping his community across India, more or less united. And the Nehru-Gandhis were the only family under whose umbrella Congressmen could remain together. Hindu domination would ruin this Dar-ul-Aman.

But subsequently, Patel caught Covid and left the mortal world. Being a non-Hindu, he easily fitted into the mould of Sonia Gandhi's preferences, who blindly trusted him. Her demands for a political advisor were very tall. Herein lay the knotty issue of the troubles the party found itself in. It is utterly bereft of any political strategy. More seriously, the ethos of India transformed from the Nehruvian to Hindu. What to do in this situation?

The Gandhi dynasty's scions, like many in the intelligentsia are vague about the changing nature of India's politics. Understandably, change brings insecurity born of the sense of uncertainty. However, politics, like nature, does not allow status quo to prevail for long.

The Congress' woes were bigger than the Gandhis' non-existent leadership. India's power structure has changed fundamentally. The Nehru-Congress was essentially a *sarkari* party, representing the bureaucratic-managerial class that ruled India. Today, the discourse is dominated by productive ideas and the culture of India's homegrown talent in enterprise. The Congress, with its overwhelming Lutyenism, understandably sees itself in a new and possibly unknown realm. It also has no answer to a formidable adversary called Narendra Modi, an entirely self-made leader, whose singular commitment is to the nation, and not any dynasty.

Why Pakistan is Tottering

Quaid-e-Azam Mohammed Ali Jinnah had presented the Muslims of British India with a bunch of interesting phrases. On the eve of the partition of India, he had said, "Once we are freed of the clutches of these Hindu banias, I promise you that we shall make Pakistan the most prosperous country in the world".

After seventy-eight years, Pakistan's Prime Minister Shehbaz Sharif says that he feels ashamed to go with a begging bowl and ask for aid from other countries. What can explain this state of affairs, a journey from the promise of prosperity to the sordid reward of bankruptcy?

Jinnah himself went to London at the age of sixteen and stayed there for four years, in the course of which he became anglicised to the extent that he had whisky and ham sandwiches. Justice M C Chagla in his popular autobiography *Roses in December* confirms that Jinnah's wife Ruttie used to lovingly bring his favourite sandwiches to office, where he enjoyed them. His younger brother Ahmed told his friend and my maternal grandfather Dharamdas Vora in Bombay that they (the Jinnahs) were culturally Parsi.

Jinnah fell out with Gandhi at the 1928 Calcutta session of the Congress; from the way Gandhi let the crowd treat him, it was clear that the latter would not be allowed to go ahead in national politics and would always have to remain a subordinate. The very thought was galling to Jinnah.

At the time of its secession from West Pakistan in 1971, the former East Pakistan had a distinctly greater population than the western wing. In fact, this was the main reason why the politicians of West Pakistan did not mind the eastern wing seceding, particularly those West Pakistani politicians with prime ministerial ambitions. The two wings were so far apart that Allama Iqbal, the poet who forcefully articulated the idea of a separate state for the subcontinent's Muslims, in his 1930 map did not include Bengal as a part of the proposed Pakistan.

Neither was Balochistan a part of Pakistan when the latter was carved out in 1947. In fact, it was not even a part of British India; it had always existed as a separate princely state and even had an embassy in Karachi. Jinnah ordered the Pakistani army to invade and annex this large state in 1948. Balochistan has remained in discontent ever since and today there is a full-blown separatist movement in the province as the Balochs want to be free of a Pakistan that has done nothing but exploit them and treat them as slaves. There is a Baloch National Army spearheading the movement.

Incidentally, on the morrow of Independence, Jinnah had requested India's first Prime Minister Jawaharlal Nehru through India's High Commissioner in Karachi, Sri Prakasa, to ensure that his magnificent house in Bombay was not demolished or sold; he proposed to visit Bombay from time to time and, if possible, come back to live there one day. The splendid house still stands in Malabar Hill in Mumbai in all its marble glory.

Could it be that this Indian social memory led Jinnah to divide India so that Hindustan remained a cosmopolitan country and did not become an Islamic republic like Malaysia or Indonesia? An undivided India today would have been about half-Muslim and half-Hindu. One should not also forget to include the erstwhile East Pakistan (which in 1971 became Bangladesh) in this canvas of a possible undivided India.

Jinnah was a unique advocate who not only pleaded and persuaded eloquently, but also induced unwilling clients into becoming enthusiastic litigants. Muslim-majority provinces like Punjab and Bengal had little interest in a partition because they were happy and comfortable in their majorities; they had their legislators, ministers and chief ministers. On the other hand, in the provinces where Muslims were in a minority, of what use was a partition going to be for them? They had to stay back in Hindustan. Yet, Jinnah was able to convince them to vote for a partition, and celebrate it as the establishment of a "New Medina". His entire advocacy, including addressing crowds of fifty thousand or more, was performed in fluent English; there was no other language he could make a speech in.

The Hindus were many more in number at the time. They were more educated, and were much more in industry and business. There was an inevitability that the government would be elected by vote and not by feudal or oligarchic means. The Muslim elite did have farmlands, orchards *et al*, but these could, like the *zamindaris*, be taken over by the government. The only traditional businessmen among Muslims were the Memons, Khojas and Bohras, who preferred competing with the Pathans and Punjabis, rather than the Banias, Parsis or Chettiars. They, therefore, preferred Partition.

Having ruled from Delhi for the best part of six centuries,

Muslims would not now like a Hindu-dominated government or polity. This was indeed articulated by none other than Sir Sayyid Ahmed Khan of Aligarh when he said that the British had no right to hand over Muslims to a people over whom they had ruled for so long.

Strangely enough, Hindus and Muslims are, in the economic context, a study in contrast. When Muslims experienced material shortages, they moved on to other lands. Hindus, on the other hand, have not been known to be invaders of other lands. They have preferred to stay at home and produce wealth. In a peculiar way, the Indian Muslims might have viewed Partition as a different form of conquest. Otherwise, what was the need to chase out as many Hindus and Sikhs as possible from Pakistan including from what is now Bangladesh? If only they had allowed Hindus to live peacefully, the business talent of the latter would have today been of great help to Pakistan in its hour of dire need.

The Sindhi Muslim leaders M A Khuhro, G M Syed and others had initially advised the Hindus of Sind to stay put even after 1947, so that Sind's economy could function smoothly. But just a few weeks after Partition, the Muslim League instructed them to get rid of Sind's Hindus, in order to make space for the Mohajirs to settle there. The Punjabi leadership of Pakistan did not want the Mohajirs and preferred only Punjabi refugees from the east of their province.

If one were to borrow from Prof Timur Kuran, a Turkish-American scholar, Muslims may be good soldiers, but are not inclined to trade and commerce. Pakistan was thus deficient in business and managerial talent. Inexplicably, Pakistan also failed to throw up effective political leadership. Consequently, there have been three long spells of military dictatorship, beginning with Field Marshall Ayub Khan, followed by General Zia-ul-Haq and later General Pervez Musharraf. Again, the Pakistani army has excelled in setting up its own businesses and commercial interests, rather than fighting bravely on the battlefields of Kashmir, Punjab or Bengal. As rulers, the Pakistanis were not able in any way to modernise the Pakistani economy or society. In fact, if anything, General Zia-ul-Haq took it back by a century or two.

Religions *per se* have to be conservative, because of what the holy book says or the prophet decrees; these have to be obeyed. Those who wrote the scriptures are not around, nor are the prophets. If the faithful wish to continue to abide by them unquestioningly, there is no way a country can move with the times. The central malady of Pakistan has been its refusal to get organised and move forward. The clergy have nursed an additional apprehension of a neighbouring India, which always talked the language of planning and progress. What helped this process was the Baghdad Pact, followed by CENTO and then SEATO in the east, followed in turn by the Soviet invasion of Afghanistan and all the American aid that flowed into Islamabad. At times, it was often claimed that the Pak economy was racing past India's. We now see that it was never so.

Lately, the Americans have not been charitable. The end of the financial aid bonanza has triggered off the crisis in Pakistan we are currently witnessing. Nor has the flirtation with China helped. All this only adds up to proving Prof Timur Kuran right, that over-dependence on religion breaks rather than accelerates the economy. We could add that the injection of foreign aid is the opium of a country's economy. Pakistan is a glaring example of this truth.

Jinnah

Beyond the normal human interest, a metaphysical question arises as to what could be the mission behind the life and career of Mohammad Ali Jinnah. A former correspondent of the Pakistani daily *Dawn* who was stationed in Delhi but now has settled in the UK, says: "Partition saved Hinduism".

We say that without Jinnah, Partition was unlikely to have been possible. There appeared to be no other leader amongst the Muslims who could either argue or negotiate with the British Viceroys and ministers. Jinnah was about the only Muslim who could do both with the taller Congress leaders like Sardar Vallabhbhai Patel and Bhulabhai Desai and of course, Jawaharlal Nehru. Nor did any other Muslim Leaguer have an all-India stature. Jinnah had the brains to think up of a tactical scheme that could lead to Partition, such as the Direct Action of July/August 1946, which convinced the British as well as the Hindus generally that an undivided India would be a scabbard with two swords. Little wonder, therefore, that Lord Mountbatten landed in Delhi to become the Viceroy, fully convinced that there was no alternative to partitioning India before the British departed.

Jinnah was a second-generation Muslim. His grandfather was one Poonjabhai Thakkar, a businessman. He was prominent enough for the Dhoraji town market, not very far from Rajkot. Yet, as often businessmen's fortunes fluctuate Poonjabhai's also dipped. On the suggestion of a friend, he diversified into fish trading. This upset his vegetarian Lohana caste. Poonjabhai could see no alternative for survival, except to stick to the trading of fish. Inevitably, the tension led to Poonjabhai's expulsion from the Lohana caste. On the rebound, Poonjabhai converted to an Ismaili Khoja, a follower of Sir Aga Khan. The discomfort of the change eventually led to the migration of the family to the port city of Karachi. His father, Jinahbhai, continued in his ancestral trade, becoming a chartered accountant from London. Jinnah's passport read "Mohammad Ali Jinabhai". He began to be known as such among the few people he met in London. He had sailed to the British Empire's capital at the age of 16. Before long, he realised that accountancy was not his cup of tea. On the suggestion of his or hostel mates he tried his hand at attending lectures and eating dinners at the Lincoln's Inn of law, which he liked. After he passed the examination called Barrister-at-Law two years later, Jinnah learnt that he was too young to be presented with his certificate. He had to wait till he attained the age of 21. During the two free years while he waited, Jinnah spent his evenings often going to the theatres that were flourishing in London, showing the plays that interested him.

The other activity Jinnah pursued was to attend sessions of the House of Commons whenever he could and assist politicians; for example, serving as a secretary of Dadabhai Naoroji, who incidentally became a Liberal Member of Parliament representing the Finsbury Constituency from 1892 to 1895. All in all, Jinnah enjoyed life in London and became a brown Englishman before he returned to India. There is little evidence that he evinced any interest in religion or matters of spirituality. His legal career became more and more dazzling as he progressed at the Bombay High Court. Many of his friends were Hindus, and he particularly enjoyed the company of high class Parsis. His brother Ahmed Ali told that the author's grandfather "Culturally we brothers are Parsi. We do not pray nor did we have suitable clothes until Mohammed was made life president of the Muslim League."

Most Muslim Congressmen were members of the League, just as many Hindu Congressmen attended the Hindu Mahasabha meetings. Until the 1928 plenary session, of the Congress in Calcutta, Jinnah was arguably the most secular politician in India. The manner in which he was treated at the 1928 session, however, his politics soured and when he left Calcutta, he told his friend Dewan Chaman Lal with tears in his eyes, "This is the parting of ways". After reaching Bombay, Jinnah began preparing to migrate to London to pursue his legal practice. He was already one of the highest paid barristers in all of the British Empire. His bitter sentiments were primarily caused by his feeling outclassed by Gandhi in mass politics. He had been used to debating and arguing in panelled chambers, not on the beaches and streets.

While Jinnah led an upper class life living in his own elegant house at Hampstead, he did miss his politics. When in 1934, Nawabzada Liaqat Ali Khan came visiting to London, he had dinner with Jinnah to propose that the Quaid-e-Azam return to India to head the League and pump life into it. The Quaid's prompt reply was that Liaqat should survey all the provincial capitals and ascertain whether the Leaguers wanted him as life president. This the Nawabzada did, and Jinnah returned to Bombay in 1935. Thereafter, the new president's mind was focused on what aim and strategy was needed for the League to be able to make its mark. In the 1937 provincial elections held, the League did not do very well; the message was—something drastic was necessary. The outcome was the well-known Pakistan Resolution, which was passed in the open session of the League on 23 March, 1940. The resolution said that "The Hindus and Muslims are, as it were, opposite communities and could not coexist in the same country." The answer, therefore, was the partition of the country into Hindustan for the Hindus and others, and Pakistan for Muslims.

The Quaid's arguments were that the Muslims were a numerical minority; they were backward, less educated and poor, and the wealthy Muslims were seldom industry captains. Since he knew only English and some Gujarati, he addressed mass meetings in English only, but yet set out to campaign for Partition. He was intelligent enough to know that the majority Muslim provinces did not need partition, for they already had de facto Muslim rule, their own chief ministers and so on. It was the minority provinces that could be left out in Hindustan in the event of Partition.

The Punjab was certainly not interested in partition; they had their Unionist Party coalition of all communities with the province's premier always being a Muslim. Bengal was somewhat similarly placed. The Sindhis were happy by themselves, especially after being separated from the large Bombay Presidency. The North West Frontier Province (NWFP) was under Congress rule and Balochistan was a princely state called Kalat. Partition, therefore, ended up by becoming an event that was for the name and fame of Jinnah and his place in history as the founder of a nation.

On Conversions

Religious conversions, always a contentious issue in Indian society, have of late become more acrimonious as a socio-political faultline. The roots of the fear of conversions among Hindus topped up by the lure of Christians and Muslims to convert are much deeper than apparent so far. Unless they are understood, accepted and resolved, Hindus will continue to look upon conversions as *jihad*. Before long, conversion to Christianity may well begin to be looked upon as love crusade and draw a similar counter-reaction, but for the Christian antipathy to polygamy. In a Hindu-Christian marriage, the former's parents need have no fear that the Christian man will marry again without divorcing his Hindu wife. Nevertheless, this is only the surface of the problem.

Hinduism, or any faith that is founded on the belief in *karma* backed by *dharma*, is a faith in which one can worship or even passively believe. Its priests or leaders do not come out to lure non-Hindus to come over to their faith, unlike Christianity or Islam. They neither force, allure or induce people to turn into Hindus. They, do not offer goodies like clothes, meals, even free education and free health care to attract others to become Christians. Nor do they have the annual proceeds of *zaikat*, to help attract new entrants to Islam.

In marketing lingo, these are facilities for pushing one's religion to lure others. Christianity and Islam are, in this context, Push faiths. In the extreme, advertising is a means of push. Offering sale schemes, more of the product free of cost or offering of gifts if the buyer bought so much quantity, etc are all means of push. The Hindu temples offer none of these freebees. At most, one takes a coconut to the deity, one may accept half of the offering back. In the Lord Jagannath temple at Puri, if a worshipper seeks blessings, he may get a few strokes of a thin twig on his shoulder by the priest. To that extent, the Hindu faith survives by pull. The message to followers, present or potential is: come for *darshan* if you want to. We have no goodies to give you nor any threat to convey if you do not come. The choice is entirely yours.

Virtually all temples are on their own except for a chain like ISKCON. Freedom is another name of Hinduism; there are no compulsive obligations. Besides, there are a hundred-odd deities to choose from to worship. On the other hand, one can be an agnostic with no need for worship of a deity. The Hindu faith is a paradise of liberty. Supposing four Hindus from the four corners of the country meet. Let us assume that the person from the south has seen only white roses; the man from the north knows roses to be only red. The eastern Indian might know only pink roses while the person from the western region of the country can perhaps conceive of only yellow roses. They would disagree and argue but eventually part on a note of agreeing to disagree. Each could say; may be in your part of the country roses are what you say. In complete contrast, the adherent of an

Abrahamic religion, be he a Jew, Christian or Muslim, will most likely insist that the particular colour of the rose he has seen and is familiar with alone is a rose, and assert that the other three flowers are actually a different species altogether, and only carry the nomenclature of a rose.

The social realm is not free of these tendencies either. Leave aside war or a crusade, mere sexual attraction often leads to marriage and conversion. There is no bar to people of two differing faiths becoming husband and wife; the children should be free to choose their faiths. Why dictate her/his religion before the child is born? This propensity to decide and dictate can and does lead to fighting which makes it difficult for two communities to coexist in one locality or even country, as Mohammed Ali Jinnah asserted on 22 March 1940 at the league session at Lahore.

Jinnah justified Partition and achieved it in 1947. More Muslims live in India than in Pakistan. In 1971, the two wings of Pakistan fell apart. Now the western wing is facing a crisis, not merely economic but an existential one as well. The world is advancing rapidly and, therefore, all societies should get busy with modernising their laws. Laws and norms drafted a millennium ago certainly deserve a relook by scholars of today, rather than going on practising antiquated and out-dated codes.

Also, modernity and progress cannot coexist with backwardness and medieval obscurantism. Tension and conflict between the two will inevitably rear their head. After all, how can a world proceeding ahead in the twenty-first century, coexist with the seventh century?

The Ideological Element in the BJP's Dominance

In all the commentary on the Bharatiya Janata Party's crushing victory in the recently concluded assembly elections in Gujarat, not many political scientists appear to have noticed that the BJP follows an ideology, namely, that of Hindudom. Hindudom, which in political parlance can be termed Hindutva, has grown out of the soil of Hindustan. It is arguably the only political idea that is home grown. The Constitution of the United States of America insists on a wall to separate the State from any religion. The American constitution allows little scope for an extended discussion on ideology.

Let's go back to the oldest continuing democracy, namely Great Britain, where the foundational principle is the rule of law, lucidly laid down in the Magna Carta of 1215 AD. Thereafter, King Henry VIII laid down that the monarch would be the head of the Church of England, a principle that still prevails. However, these are rules or principles, and not really ideological tenets. Across Europe, there was no system of evoking an ideology for the purpose of the polity, and religion was treated as the rudder of the state. The French Revolution implicitly introduced nationalism, which in turn, effectively sidelined religion as the state ideology.

'Liberty, Equality, Fraternity,' the heralding cry of the French Revolution of 1789 became the world-famous three-word slogan. No one realised that liberty and equality contradict each other. The Hindu view of life is that the accumulated *karmas* of an individual determine his future, and the *karmas* of two individuals cannot be the same. Hence, the *bhagya* or destiny of two individual too cannot be the same. The ignorance of this paradigm of life while drafting ideologies carried on into the nineteenth and twentieth centuries. Take Marxism, for example, which defines itself as "from each according to his ability, to each according to his needs". Socialism saw this as "from each according to his ability to each according to his opportunity". If one were to extend this analogy further, Marx might have defined capitalism as "from each according to his ability, to each according to his greed".

Benito Mussolini offered a third alternative between capitalism and Marxism, which supposedly stood for class exploitation and class conflict respectively. The Italian leader's ideology called Fascism was summed up as class collaboration. All these were European products, which were practised on the Continent, and also exported to Asia, Africa, South America, *et al.* China and Japan are also operating on Marxism and liberal democracy respectively. However, none of these ideologies connect with the soil, even of the nations they were born in. They are native to none of the cultures that are practising them. Less or more, there is a mismatch between belief or faith and practice.

On the morrow of independence, India adopted socialism without trying to keep its own culture in focus. The slogan was "to build a socialistic pattern of society" in the words of then Prime Minister Jawaharlal Nehru. At about the same time, Nehru declared "dynamic neutrality" as the foundation of our foreign policy. Soon thereafter, the suggestion of a foreign diplomat that non-alignment is a more chiselled term hit home and, therefore, it was adopted. Then, to reassure the minorities, especially the Muslims, 'secularism' was imported from Europe. This was nothing but Nehruvianism.

India cannot live and function without religion, therefore, secularism was explained as "freedom of religion" and "equality of all of them", whereas it has nothing to do with either. The original European concept of secularism is the complete separation of the church from the state. To illustrate, until the French Revolution, the third chamber of France's National Assembly was exclusively for abbots and bishops. Every bill had to pass through the third chamber in order to become an act. This chamber was abolished after the French Revolution.

When the Marxists came to power in Russia they shut down most of the country's churches and mosques; many were also demolished. This was an attempt to separate religion from the society. This is only to demonstrate how an ideology disconnected from the soil does strange things.

India itself demonstrated a disconnect, but in the last few years, there is a reconnect. Think of all the economic and systemic progress that has been made since 2014. Earlier, during the Nehruvian period, foreign economists laughed at us and our "Hindu rate of growth". Today, India is being spoken of as being on the highway to becoming a superpower after jettisoning the Nehruvian rate of growth.

What is the reason for this astonishing transformation? The secret evidently lies in the ideology of the current government, which understands the common reason: Indian. The Indian behaving and functioning in tune with his innate temperament and cultural ethos is obviously the larger and wider reason. But the real tale is that Indian society, which was long suppressed under the shackles of an alien and hostile ideology, has at last found the space and opportunity to express itself. That is the magic a native ideology and its vibrancy in its society can work.

Why Opposition should not be an Obstruction

Just as the art of governance is important, the craft of opposition needs to be cultivated. It is obvious that by and large, hardly any political opposition since the country's independence displayed this ability. Quite often, a session in Parliament betrays the fact that it has not realised even the fundamentals of conducting itself as an Opposition.

It often looks as if the opposition parties derive pleasure in the adjournment of parliamentary proceedings and sessions. The number of times opposition members troop into the well of the House and the rapidity with which the Speaker reacts by adjourning the House, conveys the impression that he/she has punished the unruly members. But in actuality, this is not so. For long years, we have not seen marshals being used to carry away any recalcitrant member on the Speaker's orders. How many members of the house realise that the marshals' primary function is to help maintain order in the House?

With the advent of the television inside Parliament, and the proceedings of the country's apex legislative institution being telecast live across the country, it is important to realise that every action of every Member in the House(s) of Parliament is being watched by potentially everybody in the country. Comparatively speaking, very few Members use this medium of mass communication to try and project themselves to the people of India. To the contrary, there are Members of Parliament who inform people in their constituency in advance, asking them to watch Parliamentary proceedings on a particular day, as they would be out to create a ruckus and 'show' Parliament what they're 'capable' of; in other words, playing to their respective galleries, which in this case are the voters of their constituency. However, such forced adjournments only deliver the message of truancy. They convey to the electorate that a member draws a salary plus allowances, stays in the House for an hour or hour and a half, and then provokes an adjournment. What is equally wrong is the relative emptiness of the House during the couple of hours following lunch, and often, even longer.

In the 1980s and 1990s, I knew several MPs who regularly stayed in the House and thereafter went home for a meal, to be followed by a siesta. Their side of the story was that proceedings in the House were either in English or Hindi. They were familiar with Hindi but could not understand enough English. Moreover, being from smaller towns, they were not all familiar with many of the subjects debated. They, therefore, found the proceedings boring. When I asked these MPs why they did not raise these issues as a special mention, one sharp answer was: who would listen to us? Instead, why not let us have our siesta and hopefully lengthen our lives? The same MPs could easily engage a crowd of up to fifty thousand people in their own constituencies. One of them, in the course of ten years and two terms, had a chance to participate in one starred question for a total of five minutes. Another two MPs had not even opened their mouths on the floor of Parliament during the course of these ten years.

Incidentally, one can speak in any of the national languages while speaking in Parliament, but one has to give a clear notice of a week, so that a suitable interpreter can be arranged. In this context, the problem was, and remains: how many members can understand a speech in say, Telugu, Tamil, Punjabi or Assamese?

While in the Opposition, it is the duty of political parties to highlight facts about policies and actions the government may be considering. This highlighting, however, should not amount to boycotting, browbeating or bullying, but should be done through explaining and expressing what the Opposition would do to solve the same problem, how and at what cost, if and when it were to be in power. Descending into the well and provoking an adjournment would be tantamount to running away from the field of duty. The constituents and the voters know what the alternative programme ought to be, in which case, how would the Opposition gain? The government and its ministers have the opportunity to obtain continual publicity of their point of view through all channels and media. The Opposition does not have this privilege. On the contrary, in the view of the public, the impression may be conveyed that the Opposition is not serious; its members want to collect their salaries and allowances and enjoy themselves by expending time through adjournments.

One answer is for the willing members of the Opposition to get together and organise a shadow ministry, with each member specialising in one subject, say foreign affairs, defence matters and so on. The resulting specialised knowledge would enable the Opposition to oppose the government with the authority of knowledge and logic. They would then not have to be weak politicians who fret and descend into the well of the House, raise sound and fury, but are heard no more while the government operates from its castle.

Why is there this Clamour for Reunification?

Some recent writings have spoken of the desirability of merging Pakistan with our country. That, in their opinion, is to save our neighbour from disaster. Howsoever noble sounding this might be, its implementation would be fraught with national suicide. While ardently pursuing his advocacy for a separate state for the subcontinent's Muslims, Pakistan's founder Quaid-e-Azam Jinnah had categorically declared at Lahore that "the two communities (meaning Hindus and Muslims) cannot coexist in one country". He had gone on to back up his demand with an appeal for an exchange of populations. Such an exercise had been done in 1923 by the League of Nations (predecessor of the UNO) wherein Muslims in Greece crossed over to Turkey, whose Christians shifted to Greece in an organised manner.

As it happened, only a few Muslims crossed over to Pakistan, whereas almost all the Hindus were chased out of there; the remaining being ethnically cleansed. Nevertheless, in the light of history, Partition proved to be a blessing because India's population remained in balance. In any case, the people of Pakistan have grown up under three successive constitutions, all of which confer sovereignty to Allah the Merciful.

One particular newspaper article was emphatic in its comparison with the reunification of Germany at the end of the Cold War. Such comparisons are not only misplaced, but are grossly misleading as well. For one, all Germans are the same people, virtually all of them Christian, who were torn apart by the Cold War between the West and the Soviet Union. Not a single German had demanded this partition on the morrow of WWII. Marshall Josef Stalin, the Soviet dictator, might have accepted a united Germany provided the whole of Deutschland would have come under the Soviet roof. Stalin indeed did cherish this hope which was dashed by Harry Truman, who cherished no illusions about Stalin being a reasonable partner for peace.

To return to Pakistan, Jinnah had promised the Muslims in 1946, 'Once independent and free from Hindu clutches, we will make Pakistan the most prosperous country in the world.' As an ally of the USA, aid in dollars began to pour in. When the Soviet Union invaded Afghanistan, Pakistan became an 'indispensable ally'.

Naturally, there was no shortage of aid; how much was spent on the military and how much for civil society cannot be known, as probably no accounts would be available today. However, one did get to hear of milk and honey flowing in that country in the closing years of the twentieth century. There were also reports of Pakistan's per capita GDP overtaking India's. The American withdrawal from Afghanistan has had a cataclysmic effect on the Pakistani economy because its utility as an ally has petered out.

Jinnah was a brilliant lawyer who not only pleaded effectively but could also persuade an unwilling litigant to take up a cause—in this case it was that of a separate Muslim homeland. The Muslim majority provinces like Bengal, Punjab and Sind were happy with their majorities; legislators and ministers, and always had a Muslim premier. So, why Partition?

The Muslims, in the provinces where they were in a minority, needed the security of a Muslim state, but they could not obtain this as they were in a minority. Jinnah, therefore, brought out the concept of an exchange of population from his bag of arguments. The minority Muslim population in the non-Muslim majority provinces could emigrate to the proposed New Medina. Students of the Aligarh Muslim University were very active in canvassing for a New Medina.

The last Caliphate had been abolished in 1924. Jinnah argued that the Muslims in the subcontinent would be outnumbered by the Hindus. They, i.e., the Muslims were less educated and their elite were mostly landowners, lacking industries or trade and commerce. Jinnah with his eloquence in English (he could not orate in any other language) was able to convince most of them that the challenge before them was "Pakistan or Perish".

Jinnah was an introvert who did not mix with the masses. His social circle was the Parsi and Gujarati elite, mostly of Bombay, a city which the Quaid loved dearly. He was barely familiar with Islamic theology.

All in all, Jinnah was a brown Englishman who wore expensive Saville Row suits and loved fraternising with the English. Street and *maidan* politics, which were Gandhi's forte, were not Jinnah's cup of tea. He accepted the life presidentship of the Muslim League to get even with Gandhi. Partition was a mistake, as unfolding events are proving. All Jinnah was obsessed with was his place in history, no matter what the cost.

Churn among the Christian Community

There is a greater affinity between Hinduism and Christianity than with Islam or Judaism. Jesus Christ walked the earth and performed innumerable miracles to cure and help common folk in the region around Jerusalem. His betrayal by Judas, trial by the Roman rulers and crucifixion on Calvary Hill are all on record. Christians insist Jesus was the son of God whereas the Muslims look upon him as a prophet; the Jews reject him as nobody. Hindus, who take interest in knowing about other religions, would say he was rather like an avatar.

I am a committed Hindu with clear views on my faith. When I visited Jerusalem a few years ago, I was feeling somewhat ill and weak. On our visit to the Calvary Hill, I somehow forgot about rest and simply kept going upward, with my family, till we reached the top of the hill and returned to the base and then our hotel. Evidently, some unknown and unseen power was driving me to walk on further upwards.

To come back to similarity: Christianity is not as much against idol worship as its priests might claim. Every church has a cross, while every Roman Catholic place of worship has a portrait or statue of Virgin Mary as a symbol of Immaculate Conception. Hinduism also permits the practice of *niyog*, which means surrogacy, wherein the fathers could even be celestial figures, as were the fathers of the Pandavas of the Mahabharata. Significantly, Islam and Judaism demand transnational loyalty from their followers. The Muslims call this "*qaum* above *vatan*", i.e., religion above state. On the other hand, nationalism above all, as a concept was conceived by Christian Europe. Hindus have their faith in Bharat Mata (Mother India) as the political goddess to be followed. In this context, the only point of difference in India between Christianity and Hinduism is conversion of poor Hindus. Tempting and luring needy Hindus by offering help, including money, in exchange of quitting the worship of say, Ramji and Hanuman, and worshipping Jesus Christ in a Church from day one after conversion, has been unwelcome, and also a source of tension.

A day's visit to the Dangs district of Gujarat would demonstrate the anguish local Hindus feel. The Christian community across the world comes through as well educated. And knowledge can lead to thinking; and quite a few thinking people can become hungry for their spiritual advancement. They would prefer not to be told as to what is pious and what is sinful; what is heaven and how they would be dispatched to one or the other on Doomsday, on the command of God. If religion touches base with logic, Christianity would fall on the side of Deductive Logic, which begins with an imaginary premise. For example, my god is the only god and there is no other. If one wants to go heaven, one has to go through him. For a simple person, it would be convenient to accept such a given thesis because the corollaries that follow such a thesis are easy to digest. But a thinking person may find the proposition imposing. He would welcome the freedom for his psyche to play about with, in which case, Hinduism with its inductive logic would be more satisfying. The reason is that the faith would expect the follower to choose his dharma or duty in life. Thereafter, it would be a matter of how well he works towards fulfilling that *dharma*. For the thinking psyche, it is freedom and freedom all the way. There is almost a limitless treasure of scriptures and mythology to guide the follower, from the Vedas, Puranas, Bhagavad Gita and the epics Ramayana and Mahabharata.

Fortunately, in the inter religious context, Hinduism does not have an "Other" to quarrel with. It is the deductive approach that has made many a European lose interest in Christianity. There is no animosity against it, but a loss of interest as it leads to an unfulfilled spirituality. Hinduism on the whole has not proselytised or made any real attempt to convert and yet, there are some one hundred ISKCON temple complexes, mainly in the USA and Europe. The chant of "Hare Krishna, Hare Rama" has been popularised by ISKCON.

Take for example, Kerala. Christianity simultaneously faces two rivals. There is communism along with its insistent atheism, and the sword of Islam whereas Hindus ideally prefer peace and harmony. Christianity on its own cannot wield power. The choice of the Christian community to solely depend on itself in the last elections handed the communists a thumping victory. Why should Kerala enjoy the unique honour of keeping the flag of Marx fluttering? Hardly anywhere else in the world is it even remembered. Even libraries have reduced space on their shelves for *Das Kapital*. Kerala is a cultural jewel of India. Its specialty is worship; the state's temples and churches are a unique sight to behold. The Maharaja of Travancore, when he ruled as the trustee of Lord Padmanabha, allowed up to 20 per cent of his people to become worshippers of Jesus Christ. Today, there is hardly any Christian denomination that is not present in Kerala.

Disrespecting India's Sovereignty

Is it not unfortunate that the governments of USA and Germany have commented on the compaction of Rahul Gandhi by a court of law in Surat, followed by his being disqualified from Parliament's membership? Crossing international borders to comment on happenings in another country is inappropriate diplomacy to say the least. Not minding one's business is misbehaviour. To do it at the international level is a violation of another country's sovereignty.

Germany is a very young democracy that took birth only after World War I which is when the Weimar Republic came into being, before being shoved under by the Nazis. But the American democracy is about two and a half centuries old. For the US State Department to make such a mistake is unforgivable, more so when its current President is going out of his way to laud India as an indispensable ally in Asia.

The first principle of democracy is to have deference for the views and feelings of others. Without this, democracy cannot endure. Democracy in modern times began when at Runnymede, King John of England in 1215 AD signed the

Magna Carta, establishing the concept of rule of law.

This meant that all citizens are equal before the law, which also means one citizen does not interfere in the affairs of another, unjustifiably. By the same token, one nation ought not to interfere in the affairs of another. This in turn means each country must respect the sovereignty of another. The victory in World War II showered praise on the American establishment; they felt qualified to dictate policy to the world. In 1953, the independent Iranian government asked the Anglo-Iranian Oil Company to audit their books through local auditors. The UK as well as the USA were offended at this order of the Iranian state and engineered a toppling of the nationalist government of Mohammed Mosaddegh. The Western powers replaced him with the regime of Iran's monarchy of Shah Mohammad Reza Pahlavi. This regime had to survive solely on Anglo-American support till 1979, when Ayatollah Khomeini's Revolution took place.

The next American intervention was in 1983 under President Ronald Reagan, under the pretext of protecting American nationals against a Marxist regime. The USA has also intervened militarily in Korea and Vietnam for the purpose of prevention of the spread of communism. It intervened twice in Iraq in 1991and then in 2003, overthrew Saddam Hussein, another nationalist leader in the Arab world who had defied the Americans.

One can praise the United Kingdom for having systematically developed internal democracy. But when it came to the outside world, London adopted double standards. It treated Asia and Africa as free playing fields of its imperialist designs, which led to its rise and also its fall. Britain's leaders saw no wrong in invading, ruling and exploiting other countries. The results of this double standard are there for everyone to see today.

In contrast is Germany. Not that it did not want any colonies but it failed to capture and hold any except Tanganyika for a while. Yet it achieved enough to become today the fourth largest economy in the world. In great contrast, India has kept away from imperialistic adventures. It has itself been a victim of imperial adventures from the invasion of Mohammad bin Qasim in 712 AD to its independence from imperial Britain in 1947. Yet, it continues to stand on its own as the world's fifth largest economy and the fastest growing one.

India has known democracy since ancient times. Prior to the series of foreign invasions, there were a number of republics in ancient India; notably, the Sakyas, Koliyas, Vaishali, the Ghratvikas, Mallas, Bhagyas, Kalamas and so on. However, what comes to mind the most is the very ancient Shurasena (on federacy of Mathura and later Dwarka), whose president, an elected one at that, was none other than Lord Krishna.

That Krishna was a historical figure is no longer in doubt. Dr Shobha Mukerji's work, (who taught at Lucknow University), titled *The Republican Trends in Ancient India*, published by Munshiram Manoharlal (1969), has substantiated the historicity of Krishna millennia ago. Dr Mukerji has traced the history of ancient Indian republics that co-existed with large, straddling empires though not always happily, and that of the Shūrasena Confederacy, as the Yādava republic was known. *The Republican Trends in Ancient India* has ample historical references to the existence of smaller, self-governing republics in Krishna's time and the later periods of Indian history. Krishna's leadership of his people and the existence of the Andhakas and Vrishnīs (Krishna's sub-clans) after his era are historical facts too, borne out by research in this book, which also provides a glimpse into the republican ideas on governance and statecraft.

It is difficult to overlook American history and President James Monroe's Monroe Doctrine. This theory declared that the New World or the Americas were an American garden, which could be tended only by the USA. No country from the Old World, i.e., Europe, should interfere. If and when repairs were required to the fences of any part of the garden, meaning any country in the New World, it was America's right to do so.

On Infiltration

The current times are not merely of wars and armed conflicts, but also of infiltration. Britain hosts illegal immigrants, which costs the country 8 million pounds a day merely to feed them. Due to a clash between Burma's rebels and the country's army, reportedly at least 50,000 if not a lakh Burmese have entered India and have penetrated up into Manipur and Mizoram, some up to as far as Delhi. One estimate says there are up to 175,000 illegal immigrants in the UK.

Ukrainians by the thousands have rushed into Poland over the last year and a half, while many others are knocking on Germany's doors. Being of European stock, they are not unwelcome, whereas the immigrants entering the UK are from Rwanda, and are unwanted. A third category of potential migrants are ready to flee West Bank and the Gaza strip, but they are scrupulously unwanted by even the most zealous Islamic countries.

Europe, over the last decade or more, has been talked about as possibly becoming 'Eurabia' in the near future. Yet, when many Syrians were fleeing their own country to escape bombing by their own regime, several member countries of the European Union led by then Germany's Chancellor Angela Merkel were apparently ready to welcome them. Merkel might have perhaps been moved to sympathy by her own experience as an East German whose government killed thousands of its own citizens for wanting to flee to the West.

India has suffered illegal immigrants from Bangladesh to the tune of some 20 million of the latter's citizens living illegally in India. As if this was not troubling enough, Pakistan has lately become sick with impending bankruptcy. It is reported that its not so well-off citizens survive on one meal a day. When even that meal disappears, would they not be tempted to make a dash towards the Indian border? The citizens of Pak-occupied Kashmir feel oppressed, and some of them feel that it is their right to become Indian citizens because their Maharaja (Hari Singh, the erstwhile princely ruler of Jammu & Kashmir) had acceded to India in 1947. It was the Pakistani Mujahideen who had occupied their territory forcibly. There is no counter-answer to this claim.

Books have been written on migration, some of which contend that most peoples of the world have migrated from somewhere at some stage of history. One notable book is *Migrants* by Sam Miller. India certainly attracted waves of migration over the centuries due to its prosperity compared with Central Asia. However, that does not justify further illegal entry into India.

An almost uninterrupted flow of migration into the European Union has been changing Europe's domestic politics since the last decade or even more. Today, Europe, and particularly Southern Europe is exposed and vulnerable to pressure to migration from the Middle East and North Africa, a region referred to as MENA.

Unlike the Republican Party and its leader Donald Trump, not everyone in the USA objects to migration from Cuba or Mexico. The reason may be that they are predominantly white. On the other hand, there are US citizens who realise that allowing migration from any sundry country with varying racial stock will lead to conflict. Consequently, there is a growing reluctance to further immigration. But again, there is a divide between the Republicans and the Democrats, the latter generally favouring immigration as an addition to their votebanks.

The United Kingdom, in the aftermath of World War II, allowed free immigration from their Asian colonies as well as their Caribbean ones. In recent years they have begun to regret what their predecessors did in response to their temptation to procure cheaper labour. The French experience has been bitterer, because up to 10 per cent of the immigrants into the country are Algerians whose hearts beat often in contradiction to those of the European French.

The Netherlands and Belgium are also inconvenienced by immigrants of a similar kind, while Germany has a large number of people from Turkey, who are not really welcome. Although they have been called guest workers, the truth is that once an outsider settles in a host country for a few months, it is virtually impossible to make him or her quit. Canada and Australia have virtually limitless space, and in order to expand their economies, have liberal policies on immigration. What the cost of building multiracial or multicultural societies will be, only time will tell.

A political scientist would take a political view that in

due course, two or three different communities in the same country can lead to not only social tension, but also political competition. The current clash in West Asia is not the only example. The Indian experience of 75 years ago led to a partition, whereby 35 per cent of the land area became another country. Years ago, Nigeria fought a bitter civil war between the North Muslims and Southern Biafra Christians. The Christian East Timor separated from the rest of Islamic Indonesia because of a clash of cultures. Those dealing with migrants should bear these undeniable aspects of history in mind before framing policies.

Supra-Nationalism is no Longer Acceptable

Several columns have appeared in the national press, which have cautioned New Delhi that after the current honeymoon of prosperity passes in Kashmir, some good old troubled days of pseudo-terrorism are likely to return. As of now, the valley is part of a Union Territory, not a state. There is no assembly and consequently, not much of politics. No doubt, the prolific tourism seen in the last two years, plus the developments such as the coming of malls, cinemas and expansion of railways have all helped distract the attention of the 'moderate' separatists. All these factors have led to the current peaceful atmosphere, which some column writers have chosen to call a "current truce".

If this be true, a substantive reason for this would be a big gap in communication between the Indian state and its Muslim populace. Islam accords little importance to nationalism, unlike Christianity, under whose jumbo umbrella nationalism grew. So much so that it replaced Christianity itself as a political ideology. It was nationalism that eventually defeated and uprooted communism in early 1990. The appeal of the Communist Manifesto slogan, "Workers of the world unite" was over. Leon Trotsky's thesis was permanent revolution, which meant that there was no need to attend to any nation until the last member of the world's proletariat was unchained. The belief of the communist ideologues was that the nation is an enemy of the working class. Similarly, for its own reasons, Islam has never been interested in the nation, and is, therefore, either indifferent or hostile to *vatanparasti* (loyalty to nation). The Prophet's religion has consistently promoted *majahabparasti* (loyalty to religion) as a total prescription for an ideal life. In the bargain, a number of Muslim leaders have preferred the expression 'Muslim Indian' to 'Indian Muslim', implying religion before nation, not nation before religion.

The late Muslim leader Syed Shahbuddin would argue, till the cows came home, that he was right in saying "Muslim Indian". Chaim Weizmann, leader of the World Jewish Conference and later the first President of Israel in 1948, emphasised a similar concept when he said: "There are no American Jews, British Jews, Russian Jews, German Jews or French Jews. There are Jews in America, Jews in Britain, Jews in France, Jews in Germany and Jews in Russia".

The Jews have consistently been supra-national, which is one of the reasons many Christians of Europe have suspected them of being anti-national, whenever Jewish interests have clashed with national ones. The classic example was Adolf Hitler's repeated assertion that it was the Jews who helped defeat Germany in World War I. How and why did Germany surrender to the Western allies while German troops were still standing on French soil?

In India, the Khilafat Committee, incidentally presided over by Mahatma Gandhi, declared that if Afghanistan were to invade India, Muslim soldiers would not fight to defend

India. This prohibition covered all potential Muslim invaders. This obscurantist injunction was later affirmed by the Muslim League. This principle was later applied and quoted by the then Pakistan cricket captain Wasim Akram in the nineties. When his team lost to Bangladesh in the 1996 Cricket World Cup, Akram said to a journalist that he had no problem "losing to a brother Muslim team".

In all probability, the Islamic proclivity to supra-nationalism has not even occurred to most Muslims. They haven't been told, nor explained the reasons for it. Indian political leaders have a duty to clarify this publicly to Muslims, so that they realise why, they are suspect when it comes to their national loyalty. The moment a Muslim is seen applauding a stylish shot played by a Pak batsman, Hindus often take this to be a symptom of pro-Pakistani sympathy. The British do not react in this manner when they see a Briton of Indian origin applauding a boundary hit by an Indian batsman in an India-England match.

This psycho-syndrome is relevant in the context of Kashmir for both Muslims and Hindus—for Hindus, so that they are not perpetually suspicious; for the Muslim in the Valley to realise that their conduct can be prejudicial to their co-religionists in the rest of India. The fact that the Muslims of India with their families have been resident here, out of their own choice is not insignificant. Whatever political parties say or claim has only passing significance. The fact is that India is a majority Hindu state. Any normal person would like to be a welcome citizen rather than a suspect. Therefore, all his/her actions ought to be acceptably patriotic and not doubtful in the eyes of the majority.

The Hindus also want to feel that their co-citizens are good and loyal. To be perpetually suspecting others is no way to be happy. It is, therefore, important for the community's leaders to candidly articulate the factual situation, rather than say one thing and mean quite another.

There are several patriotic Muslims, as proved by Brigadier Usman (1948, Kashmir Valley), Havaldar Abdul Hamid in the 1965 war against Pakistan, and many others. On a macro scale could Bangladesh have attained its independence from Pakistan had India not intervened? But these sacrifices in blood are forgotten when it comes to episodes like sporting contests and diplomatic and political standoffs.

Sir Syed Ahmad Khan

We are in the season of observing the 125 years of the passing of Sir Syed Ahmad Khan, and it is perhaps an appropriate opportunity to enumerate all that his community needs to do to catch up with its comparable Hindu fellow citizens of the country. They, meaning the Muslims, cannot expect to live forever in India as a minority existing on its own terms, oblivious to advanced education, skills as well as the march of modernity. They also owe quite a few debts to the nation. These cannot be kept pending forever.

The first thing the Muslims need to do is to embrace modern education. They cannot go on hiding behind orthodoxy and make do with madrasa education for ever. They cannot be in a position where they make no serious effort to become employable and then complain of unemployment. It is heartening to note that Muslim girls appear to take to education spontaneously, although their parents may or may not have particularly encouraged them.

Whether these educated girls will continue to tolerate polygamy is a matter of conjecture. If they do not, so much the better. The community must give up the habit of claiming to be poor and backward. The message should be that it is a matter of shame for a community that claims that it has ruled India for centuries, to say so. In fact, they should have been the leaders of society rather than continually berating their own backwardness.

Let us now turn to the debts the community owes to the rest of Indians. About 9.4 lakh acres of urban land belongs to waqfs across the country; this needs urgent attention. The former chancellor of the Jamia Millia University Hakim Ajmal Khan had called the waqfs a "dead hand, unproductive and a waste of national assets". As has happened in many Muslim countries, these lands can either be surrendered voluntarily or else nationalised. Then there is the question of Hindu temples desecrated and forcibly converted into mosques. They need a solution. Not all of them can be perhaps returned, but in consultation with prominent Hindu leaders, these places of worship can and should be gracefully surrendered. Such a gesture would earn the community the enormous goodwill of the Hindus. Many a Muslim may not realise that unlike his mosque, the Hindu temple is not a mere prayer hall, but a residence of God, where the devotee hopes to one day gain a glimpse of the divine. Such spirituality and the quest for it is encouraged among Hindus.

It is, therefore, difficult for a non-Hindu to imagine the pain and agony a Hindu undergoes when he comes across a desecrated or destroyed temple. A rectification is essential, if Hindus and Muslims are to live cordially. The government, too, has to play its role in this regard, in order to abolish its practice and habit of taking over the management of Hindu temples. This is wrong and discriminatory, since mosques and churches do not come under their purview. It is a constitutional obligation to ensure that the Hindu is not discriminated against in his own country.

There is another glaring discrimination against the Hindu community for which the government alone is responsible. In schools and colleges/universities, there are reservations for the less advantaged castes. The minority institutions do not have to suffer this sacrifice induced by legislation. For electoral reasons, political parties have been constantly soft on minorities, who have come to regard these concessions incorporated into the Indian constitution when it was framed, as unalterable rights for all times to come. It is not necessary to iterate here the grievances this has given rise to in the Hindus, which of course is hardly a positive sign for the healthy functioning of our democracy.

It all began with Jawaharlal Nehru being appointed—and not elected—as president of the Congress in 1946. Mahatma Gandhi did him this favour, although Nehru did not have a real base within the party, unlike Sardar Vallabhbhai Patel. As a result, Nehru had to go out of his way to favour minorities. In the bargain, he had Articles 25 to 30 inserted in the Constitution. These Articles are in direct contradiction with the basic principles of the document, which otherwise went out of its way to emphasise the equality of all, especially Article 14. Ironically, the Nehru-inserted Articles allow certain Indian citizens to marry up to four wives at a time, but the wife cannot marry more than one husband at a time. No modern society and country can put up with polygamy, and it is for the community to come forward and voluntarily ask for its abolition, rather than wait for a legislative and political blow to fall upon it.

The Mahua Moitra Affair

At the midnight of Independence, Prime Minister Jawaharlal Nehru declared that India had woken to a tryst with destiny.

Much earlier, Mahatma Gandhi wrote a book called *Ram Raj*. The Hindu Mahasabha dreamt of building a Hindu Rashtra, while the Muslim League went out to create a New Medina in Pakistan. These were the ideals with which Indians had fought for freedom.

At last, after seventy-eight years we Indians have a Prime Minister who is building the country on the principles of *Sabka Saath, Sabka Vikas, Sabka Vishwas and Sabka Prayas.* He has led the country to become the fifth largest economy in the world, landed India on the moon with our Chandrayan and propelled the country to become a superpower.

On the other hand, there are Members of Parliament like Mahua Moitra who have done their best to drag the Parliament lower, selling even the august body's private identities like secret e-mail for perfumes, wines, handbags, free holidays, house repairs and what not. She has blackmailed an industrialist who has done no wrong. The casus belli of Moitra's ceaseless and unproven allegations against Gautam Adani, on behalf of her businessman friend Hiranandani, was that both had been competing to build and manage the Mumbai airport. Adani won the prize whereas Hiranandani failed to do so; hence his animus towards Gautam Adani. There may be other projects too, for which there could have been competition between the two.

Moitra also happens to be an MP who represents a constituency that is the headquarters of the ISKCON—namely, the town of Mayapur. Having studied and lived in the USA, she should have known what an entrepreneur means to an economy. That is precisely the role which Gautam Adani has been performing in the Indian economy very successfully. As part of the international conspiracy, Hindenburg tried to smear Adani and his group of companies but failed. As if that were not enough, Moitra has been anxious to trap an above-board Prime Minister of the integrity and stature of Narendra Modi. An educated lady like Moitra should have known that Modi is the country's Prime Minister and not of the Bharatiya Janata Party alone.

Has it not occurred to Mahua Moitra that civilisations have endured because generally, good has triumphed over evil? Shri Rama, also known and eulogised as *Maryada Purushottam* after marching across the subcontinent from north to south, annihilated the epitome of evil that that was Ravana. Imagine how history would have changed for the worse had Shri Rama lost. The more evil that prevails, the shorter is the life of the particular society. An example we are able to witness graphically is that of our neighbour Pakistan. The country has resorted to promoting schools that teach children how to execute theft. Similarly, the Pandavas ended the saga of the Kauravas. On the other hand, had the Pandavas lost, it was feared by Shri Krishna that they would not have been able to keep foreign invaders out of Bharat and this grave threat would have lasted for centuries together. Various Greek gods have appeared on earth from time to time to defeat and slay evildoers, while various Hindu avatars incarnate to defeat and put down *adharma*. The free world had united to end monstrosities like Nazism in World War II; these are all instances of this eternal phenomenon.

Although popularly elected to Parliament, Mahua Moitra obviously does not realise that the august house that gives its government and administration, is at the helm of 20 per cent of India. That is what she has profaned.

It was just about a century ago that the legendary Gopal Krishna Gokhale had declared, "What Bengal thinks today, India thinks tomorrow". That the Bengal of Gurudev Rabindranath Tagore, Bankim Chandra Chattopadhyay, Netaji Subhas Chandra Bose, who thought nothing of giving up his life for the country's freedom, or the great scientist Jagdish Chandra Bose should produce the likes of Mahua Moitra is an embarrassment to the state's history. She symbolises an attack on all that Bengal personifies.

What has not yet been noticed is the potentially ruinous impact Ms Moitra's conduct could have on the popular image of an MP in particular and politicians in general. As it is, what Moitra has done could be a big blow especially coming from a lady. Imagine the fate of democracy in India if the common folk lose all faith and respect for the members in parliament, and in turn, their ministers.

Make Voting Compulsory

Compulsory voting is an effect of laws requiring eligible citizens to register and vote in elections, and impose penalties on those who fail to do so. Presently, twenty-two countries provide for compulsory voting, and eleven democracies—about 5 per cent of all United Nations members—enforce it.

Athenian democracy held that it was every citizen's duty to participate in decision making, but attendance at the assembly was voluntary. Sometimes there was some form of social opprobrium for those not participating. Belgium has the oldest existing compulsory voting system. Compulsory voting was introduced in 1893 for men and in 1948 for women, following universal female suffrage. Belgians aged eighteen and over and registered non-Belgian voters are obliged to present themselves in their polling station. If they fail to vote in at least four elections, they can lose the right to vote for ten years. Non-voters also might face difficulties getting a job in the public sector.

Australia introduced compulsory enrolment for voting at federal elections in 1912. Voting for indigenous Australians was introduced in 1949, but enrolment and having one's name marked on the voting register was not compulsory for indigenous Australians until 1984. Venezuela and the Netherlands are countries that have moved from compulsory voting to voluntary participation. The last compulsory Dutch and Venezuelan elections were in 1967 and 1993, respectively.

Compulsory voting is increasingly resented by citizens in some countries such as Brazil. At the last presidential election in 2014, some 30 million voters, about 21 per cent of registered voters, did not vote, despite the fact that Brazil has some of the most severe penalties enforced against non voters.

It was a phenomenal initiative for India to launch its democracy with universal adult franchise on the morrow of independence. It has to be borne in mind that in 1947, up to 80 per cent of our people were illiterate. Our country was predominantly rural, with many a village not easy to drive into. North India had been drenched with blood between 1946 and 1948. Partition, in any case, had a disrupting effect not only on people but also on the administration. Hindus did not have the experience of governance at the top for the best part of nine centuries. As for voting rights for citizens, even the United Kingdom, widely accepted as the mother of modern democracies, introduced cent per cent adult male voting as late as 1918; women were granted the right to vote only by 1928.

Sardar Vallabhbhai Patel had a pragmatic mind. Universal adult franchise had been announced as part of the electoral policy. It is more than likely that the Sardar would have gone to the logical conclusion of such a franchise, that is the introduction and implementation of compulsory voting. In everything he managed, he was thorough. For example, the integration of princely states into India was so thoroughly done that all of them except Hyderabad were committed to accede to India by Independence Day. Patel could not do anything about Jammu & Kashmir since Jawaharlal Nehru had taken charge of the state, he being originally a Kashmiri; Sheikh Abdullah was his close friend.

There are several other countries that practise compulsory voting. Argentina since 1912; Australia since 1924; Brazil, Eucador (since 1936); Peru (since 1933), Uruguay (since 1970) and Singapore are among the prominent ones. If Sardar Patel did not have enough time to implement such a policy, his pragmatic successors could have done so. It is only that party which favours a votebank, which would disapprove of compulsory voting because that would make tactical voting meaningless.

This is of particular significance for India, the world's largest democracy. We have been plagued by the phenomenon of what we refer to as the votebank, particularly the "minority votebank". Put simply, this refers to the religious minority communities voting in large numbers whereas the majority Hindu community is usually either disinterested in voting or does not take much interest in political issues, but feels aggrieved when policies are not to its liking. The situation has seen a significant change after the 2014 elections, but by no means can we assert that political consciousness has come to the majority of the country's voters.

Politics that is servile to the votebank, especially of the religious nature, is also a serious long-term security threat to the nation, something India has experienced in previous decades. Cross-border terror attacks instigated by our neighbouring country with impunity were allowed to remain unpunished because of the fear that retaliatory action might aggrieve voters belonging to a particular religion thereby hurting the ruling party's prospects in future elections. This led to India justifiably being known as a soft state and, therefore, brought us little or no global sympathy in the face of unrelenting terror. Only after the 2014 elections have we seen a sea change in both voting behaviour and government policies emanating thereof. That makes the case for compulsory voting even stronger.

Repeated Destruction at Mathura

The richly jewelled idols taken from pagan temples were transferred to Agra and there placed beneath the steps leading to the Nawab Begum Sahib's mosque, in order that they might ever be pressed underfoot by the true believers. The city's name was changed to Islamabad. Can you guess the name of this unfortunate place? Vincent A Smith ICE, CIE, the famous historian brought out this historical truth.

If you cannot guess, it was Mathura, the birthplace of Shri Krishna. Most of the idols were from the just destroyed Kesava Deva mandir, built at the spot where Krishna was believed to have been born some 3,400 years ago. If Mahmud of Ghazni was a barbarian, one might have been inclined to excuse him. But both Al-Biruni and Utbi, who were chroniclers and lived in Ghazni's times, certified that Mahmud was devout and built beautiful mosques in his Ghazni.

What was perpetrated at Mathura, is unthinkable in any context of civilisation. From Jammu in the north to Kanyakumari in the south, from Dwarka in the west to Imphal in the east, there are any number of Krishna worshippers. He gave us the Bhagavad

Gita. Even today, every Hindu swears by it before answering in any court, just as Christians and Muslims swear by the Bible and the Quran respectively. If there is any one book from which a Hindu wishes to understand his faith, it is the Gita. In fact, everyone, at least in India, understands what Shri Krishna means to the Hindu psyche. Just as Sri Ram exemplifies the uncompromising idealist, Krishna personifies the comprehensive realist.

In *Mathura: A District Memoir*, F S Growse has recorded his exhaustive survey and research about *Brajbhoomi*. He was so overwhelmed by the vandalism that visited the area repeatedly that he wrote feelingly. To quote:

> Thanks to Muhammadan intolerance, there is not a single building of any antiquity either in the city itself or its environs. Its most famous temple—that dedicated to Kesava Deva (Krishna)—was destroyed in 1669, the eleventh year of the reign of the iconoclast Aurangzeb (also known as Alamgir). The mosque erected on its ruins is a building of little architectural value.

Mahmud of Ghazni was however the first iconoclast to vandalise Mathura. That was in 1017 AD about which Growse wrote:

> If any one wished to construct a building equal to it, he would not be able to do so without expending a hundred million dinars, and the work would occupy two hundred years, even though the most able and experienced workmen were employed. Orders were given that all the temples should be burnt with naphtha and fire and levelled with the ground. The city was opened to plunder for twenty days. Among the spoils are said to have been five great idols of pure gold with eyes of rubies and adornments of other precious stones,

> together with a vast number of smaller silver images, which, when broken up, formed a load for more than a hundred camels. The total value of the spoils has been estimated at three millions of rupees; while the number of Hindus carried away into captivity exceeded 5,000.

Today Bal Krishna is worshipped in a little room which appears like a servant quarter attached to the back of the mosque. Pathos can be experienced by any visitor, whether a devotee or otherwise.

To go back to Aurangzeb, over two centuries after the desecration, Growse felt that:

> Of all the sacred places in India, none enjoys a greater popularity than the capital of Braj, the holy city of Mathura. For nine months in the year, festival follows upon festival in rapid succession and the ghats and temples are daily thronged with new groups of way-worn pilgrims. So great is the sanctity of the spot that its panegyrists do not hesitate to declare that a single day spent at Mathura is more meritorious than a lifetime passed at Banaras.
>
> Not only the city of Mathura, but with it, the whole of the western half of the district has a special interest of its own as the birthplace and abiding home of Vaishnava Hinduism. In the neighbourhood is Gokul and Brindaban, where the divine brothers Krishna and Balram grazed their herds.

To paraphrase William Shakespeare, not all the scents of Arabia would suffice to wash away the sins of Ghazni and Alamgir at Mathura. And since it is not possible to claim back what was destroyed long ago, the return of the mosque and the purification of Krishnajanmabhoomi or the birthplace of Krishna, is the only alternative.

Ayodhya

In Ayodhya, the agitation in the final stages was led by the Vishwa Hindu Parishad (VHP). However, what happened on December 6, 1992, was piloted from Lucknow as well as by New Delhi.

The ministry in Lucknow belonged to the Bharatiya Janata Party (BJP), while the centre had a minority government of a grand coalition. The Prime Minister incidentally, was a Congressman. He has gone down in history as one of the best leaders of independent India, especially for revolutionising the national strategy for economic growth. Moreover, the then Prime Minister cooperated like none other, with the then UP government, on 6 December.

A lady IPS officer told me on the terrace of what was referred to as *Sita Ki Rasoi*, about 200 metres from the then Babri edifice that the police were not to interfere unless a human life was in serious danger. According to her, there were in Faizabad, four kilometres away about 15,000 jawans and officers of the Central Reserve Police Force (CRPF). Incidentally, she happened to add that there were many bulldozers and earth moving machines in the area.

As is well known, the ministry at Lucknow was dismissed at 5.30 pm the same day; the news was announced in the evening news by 6 pm. Thereafter, there was Governor's rule in UP for months together. Anything done or undone in the state, was at the behest of the Central Government. The Union Home Minister of India, according to the contemporary newspapers was in the picture regarding the happenings of the day in Ayodhya. The Union Home Minister Secretary however, was in his office but was not informed about Ram Lalla's ad hoc residence. This upset him deeply enough to eventually take premature retirement. Having been a classmate of mine at Elphinstone college, Bombay, between 1954 and 1956, he confided to me that no telephone calls were made to him that day. In fact, the happenings in Ayodhya were kept secret to the extent that I have not seen any photograph of the Babri edifice without its domes, nor have I come across anyone else who reported seeing them. The only witnesses are likely to be the people who were present at Ayodhya that day.

Any development with regard to the edifice after 5.30 that day was under the direction of the governor of Uttar Pradesh, which means that the complete demolition of the enormous structure, and the scrupulous removal and disappearance from Ayodhya of the rubble within 60 hours, was done after 5.30 pm on December 6. By 6 pm on that day, itself,, Lord Rama was virajmaan in the makeshift tent placed nearby. According to contemporary journals, Rs.9,000 in coins had been offered outside the now sacred tent, most possibly by the CRPF personal as well as some residents of Ayodhya, who had the courage to stir out of their homes.

All the local arrangement were obviously made by the

government in Lucknow. Chief Minister Kalyan Singh openly declared, "We have delivered what we promised". The men who brought down the domes were apparently trained hands of the Public Works Department (PWD). Most of them had crowbars in their hands, which they used to strike at the edge where the domes met the walls. If half the edges were to be separated, the domes would collapse. Evidently, experienced hands were necessary to execute the demolition. Political activists are seldom equipped to meet such a challenge. I would not have known all this from the distance of over 200 metres, but for the two photographer journalists who came up to the terrace to complain to the politicians above, of how badly they had been treated. They had several blood marks on their faces. I was one of the few who was comfortable speaking in English. These young men therefore, spoke mostly to me. They had ventured near the edifice to click pictures from close. They had presumed that the *kar sevaks* would love to be photographically publicised demolishing the Babri structure. When they objected to the photographers' cameras, the photo-journalists initially did not take them seriously. When the workmen's folded hands and requests did not prevent the photographers, the cameras were snatched and dashed to the ground. The scuffles were violent and caused the photographers to bleed. I was fortunate to have this pictorial description of what was happening from these two photo-journalists and from a senior lady police official. Otherwise, a 200-metre distance would have been too long to learn of all this.

It were these photographers who also told me that about half a dozen foreign correspondents had been led away by the local police earlier in the morning and had been locked in a temple for their safety. The correspondents readily acceded to the police's request, unlike the five Indian photographers.

The three domes crashed separately; the first at 2.30 pm, the second at 3.40 pm and the last at 4.30 pm. By 5 pm, it had become pitch dark. I returned to Lucknow by 9 pm on that fateful day.

Hindus Failed to Communicate Clearly

Prime Minister Narendra Modi, while inaugurating the Swarved *mandir* in Varanasi on 18 December 2023, called for the restoration of cultural symbols hit by invading tyrants. The Babri edifice at Ayodhya was arguably the beginning of such a reconstruction.

It took the Hindus forty-five years after independence before making a serious attempt to recover Lord Rama's birthplace whereas a proud and self-respecting nation should have retrieved it within three or four years after becoming free. That the Hindus did not display their pride early enough was not only a case of delayed awareness, but also a matter of poor communication.

That the Muslims did not handover the birthplace of Lord Ram meant that they did not realise how serious a matter it was for the Hindus. The latter have seldom communicated that to them a temple is a residence of the divine. It is far more sacred than a mosque or church, which are only prayer halls. They can be shifted about without causing outrage. In fact, in Europe, churches are known to be even sold. A big church in

Leicestershire was sold to the local Jain community, which then replaced it with its own temple.

Not many Muslims realise that when a temple is desecrated a Hindu is mortally hurt, unlike the demolition of a prayer hall. Surely, it is the duty of a Hindu to clarify this, loud and clear. Instead, he prefers to indulge in litigation and long legal battles.

Well before demanding Partition, Mohammad Ali Jinnah had made it clear to all Indians that Hindus and Muslims cannot co-exist in the same country. On March, 1940, he told the Muslim League members at Lahore that notwithstanding a thousand years of close contact, nationalities, which were very divergent, at any time cannot be expected to be transformed into one nation merely by the method of subjecting them to a democratic constitution and holding them forcibly together by the unnatural and artificial means of a British parliamentary statute. What the unitary government of India had failed to achieve in 150 years could not be realised by the imposition of a central federal government. It is inconceivable that the fiat or the writ of a government so constituted can ever command willing and loyal obedience throughout the subcontinent by various nationalities, except by means of the armed force behind it.

It is extremely difficult to appreciate why our Hindu friends fail to understand the real nature of Islam and Hinduism. They are not religions in the strict sense of the word, but are, in fact, different and distinct social orders. It is a dream that the Hindus and Muslims can ever evolve a common nationality. This notion of one Indian nation is the cause of most of our troubles and will lead India to destruction if we fail to revise this misconception in time. The Hindus and Muslims have different religious philosophies, social customs and literatures. They neither intermarry nor eat together and, indeed, they belong to two different civilisations which are based mainly on conflicting ideas and conceptions. Their views on life and of life are different. It is also quite clear that Hindus and Muslims derive their inspiration from different sources of history.

As the rush of Hindu refugees from East Bengal after Partition was continually rising, even till 1948, Dr Shyama Prasad Mukherji accompanied by Dr Rajkumari Amrit Kaur rushed to see Gandhi. Their mission was to appeal to the great man to accept Jinnah's proposal for an exchange of populations. Gandhi rejected this appeal categorically by stating that Partition was on 'territorial' lines and not on 'religious' grounds. What an astounding thing to say! As a result, most Hindu leaders were hesitant in telling the people that Pakistan was for Muslims and Hindustan was for others. This meant that all communal issues stood settled and India was now predominantly a Hindu country.

On the contrary, the repeated use of the word 'secular' has confused the Muslims to this day. They, therefore, do not feel embarrassed at holding on to sacred properties that were wrongly and forcibly acquired from the Hindus. Didn't the Hindus fail to communicate clearly and properly?

Adani, Dharavi and Poverty Alleviation

That industrialist Gautam Adani should find time to write an article on Dharavi (Mumbai) is surprisingly welcome. It is clear he is driven not solely by profit but also social consciousness. Nevertheless, my intention in submitting this comment is to appeal to readers not to place unfair hurdles in the path of progress of such entrepreneurs in a misplaced enthusiasm for socialism or any similar ideologies. We belong to a land where most of the people believe that one's *karma* pilots life and creates the person's *bhagya* or destiny. That being so, the European thinking is that God made man and woman equal and it is society that makes them unequal. Society's leaders have to work towards bringing back equality, but society's leaders in India shouldn't be endeavouring to bring about forced equality. They cannot, as they are unable to control or even influence the *karmas* of people at large.

The French proclaimed liberty, equality and fraternity, but liberty and equality are contradiction in terms. If equality is to prevail, there is no place for liberty. No one can curtail anyone's freedom to perform excellent karma which in turn, should inevitably result in good fortune. If Adani succeeds in recreating Dharavi, how can a competitor or any Opposition party keep down the *bhagya* of the recreator? The poverty in many parts of our country till recently was an unbearable sight and yet, except for Kerala and West Bengal, the Indian people did not get tempted by communism. They did not flirt with Fabian socialism to any significant extent and eventually gave it up. And as luck would have it the entire world virtually gave up all shades of Marxism. To a Hindu, it is a proof that *karma* is a far more superior explanation of life than the materialistic interpretation of history.

Communism and socialism are opposed to private wealth and the very idea of enterprise. But Gandhi, who rejected Marxism, had his own thinking on wealth. According to his theory of trusteeship, the wealthy people should consider their property as something God has trusted them to manage as trustees for the benefit of the poor. This theory legitimises the positions of capitalists and landlords in society, as long as they behave as trustees.

For those wondering why one of India's top industrialists who is among the world's wealthiest men should bother himself with redeveloping the world's biggest slum cluster, a look at evidence around the world should convince us. Central America remains one of the world's most violent regions, where about 4.5 per cent of the world's homicides occur, though the region has only about 0.5 per cent of the world's population. Thanks mainly to increased security efforts by the region's governments, homicide rates are down since 2015. But increased policing and security isn't the only factor responsible for this change. During this time, economic activity also increased in the "Northern Triangle" countries of El Salvador, Guatemala, and

Honduras. It is clear that favourable economic conditions help keep future crime at bay. Consistent improvement in standard of living is key to sustaining crime reduction. Inversely, it is also true that economic deprivation is detrimental for social and also national security.

Businesses and businessmen like Adani can address this by creating the infrastructure necessary for providing skills training and financing options to disadvantaged people and communities. Providing women with economic opportunities is another way for companies to help alleviate poverty. If women are trained to be entrepreneurs, they can achieve financial stability independent of their husbands. In the event their husbands are unable to work, they can continue providing for their families, and their children's quality of life will not be compromised. The present Dharavi has all of these issues that need to be addressed.

Economist Robert Shiller, a Nobel Laureate, in 2013, had warned that income inequality is the greatest source of financial risk for the twenty-first century. Many parts of the world are marked by such inequalities, while within countries, clusters like Dharavi, while contributing significantly to business and activity, continue to suffer socioeconomic inequality and appalling human living conditions. Average incomes in some Indian cities have reached first-world levels, while, in others, they resemble the poverty levels of Africa. Passing on responsibility for eradicating poverty to the government alone overlooks the role that companies can and should play in this regard. Broadly speaking, the corporate world has the task of growing the economy.

It is true that cities in countries like China are free of any slums, of the kind one sees in India's cities, but do most people know at what enormous social and political cost this is brought about? No Chinese resident of a rural area can visit the big cities without the permission of his/her regime, and that too for a specific period. While reams can be written on this, it is sufficient to conclude here that such stifling of social freedom is a threat to the prosperity and even the country's integrity a regime tries so hard to enforce.

Human freedom alone can promote wealth and prosperity; it is an unbeatable engine of technological and economic growth. As an example, one may look at the lives of countless entrepreneurs, Indian and overseas, who have wealth to not only pull themselves out of poverty, but also improve millions of lives.

Truth—a Must for Reconciliation

For any society or civilisation to flourish, long spells of peace are needed, especially internal peace. The visionary Nelson Mandela appointed a Truth and Reconciliation Commission after apartheid rule was ended in South Africa, to make sure that the bitter memories of apartheid and ill-treatment of the black people by whites, who were essentially invaders and occupiers, were forgotten, as far as possible. India has much to learn from Mandela's example and the country needs permanent internal peace. This is unlikely to be established unless bitter memories etched in concrete by the invading settlers who occupied large parts of the country linger on.

South Africa suffered apartheid for nearly four centuries; India's experience has been twice that, seven or more centuries. The African experience has few concrete reminders except perhaps statues of some white rulers, whereas India has thousands of standing mosques that were originally temples. Some were converted overnight from temples to mosques for those believing in one exclusive god. Many others were demolished to their plinth and rebuilt with the resultant debris. This is not the same as converting a church into a mosque or vice versa, because both are simply prayer halls. A Hindu temple is a residence of the divine.

A Hindu is not forbidden from trying to visualise, see or mingle with the divine; a temple and a platform for it, is one of the pathways to spirituality. A mosque, church or synagogue are merely prayer halls, a room for paying obeisance to an unseen and unseeable God. The Third of the Ten Commandments states: "Thee shall not make any gravel image of thy Lord the God". Hinduism encourages divine idols to enable the worshipper to focus on his worship. The Muslims did not understand what cruelty they were inflicting by destroying and desecrating Hindu temples. Generation after generation has come and gone since Mahmud of Ghazni demolished the famous Somnath Temple.

Of late, we hear from some quarters that Partition was ill-conceived. We humans cannot say which *dushkarma* (evil deed) is the cause of which *durbhagya* (ill fate), but believe that desecration and demolition of Hindu temples has had a great deal to do with the ill fate of the subcontinent's Muslims. Perhaps the sins of the past, especially the destruction of Hindu temples, should be atoned for by the appointment of a commission for truth and reconciliation, as in post-apartheid South Africa.

Such a commission should comprise of respected experts in archaeology and history, to bring about reconciliation between the concerned communities. While the number of temples destroyed, desecrated and converted by the Islamic invaders and iconoclasts is in thousands, noted historian and analyst Sitaram Goel had identified 3,000 prominent ones throughout the country, noted for their size, and historical and archaeological significance, apart from civilisational and religious importance for Hindus.

It is also important to stress here that the purpose of such a trust is not to seek retribution for the wrongs of the past, but to enable the nation to move on in a spirit of reconciliation. The community that follows the faith the medieval invaders belonged to must be encouraged to admit the grievous wrongs committed in the name of their faith, and voluntarily relinquish whatever claim they have on old Hindu places of worship. Of the 3,000 and more temples, 100 or 150 of the most important ones can be taken up for being handed over to the Hindu community immediately through a competent agency notified by the commission. While the commission might include a couple of the members from the highest level of the country's judiciary, it is important to lay down that the findings and conclusions of this truth and reconciliation commission should not be justiciable, i.e., open to being challenged in courts, as this would only mean dragging the issue for many years giving one side a false sense of victory while increasing the bitterness of the deprived side. Such a scenario is hardly conclusive to national harmony and the country's future. This has to be fully and finally accepted by all communities concerned.

The problem appears to be a continuing phenomenon. By August 2023, Mathura was experiencing this problem. The Railways are endeavouring to regain their legally owned land, incidentally, near the Krishna Janmasthan. One hundred and thirty five illegal shanty houses have been demolished leaving families staying there homeless. They claim they were living there for about a hundred years and have currently moved to some ad hoc tents, while approaching the Supreme Court for a stay. Another place of brewing contention is in New Delhi at a crossing called Sunehri Bagh, which became an important crossing after the Central Vista and New Parliament House were built. Earlier, there was an old grave upon which a small mosque was built, or constructed after the road crossing came into being. Over the last 42 years or so, it has become large enough to cover the entire crossing island. The New Delhi Municipal Committee has now asked the crossing to be vacated. Here again, the matter is in the court.

Ayodhya and Hindu Renaissance

For Hindus, Ramchandra or Sri Rama is not only an avatar of the divine, but also a shining example of various virtues to worship. Even for Muslims, in the words of the poet Allama Iqbal, Rama was "Imam-e-Hind" or the Prophet of India. Yet, the British Raj perpetuated the humiliation meted out to Him by the followers of the Mughal invader Babar, who desecrated the ancient temple at His birthplace in Ayodhya, from where He also ruled as the king of Awadh. To the shame of Hindus, even the first five Prime Ministers of independent India chose to continue with the perpetuation of this humiliation. It was in late 1992 that the structure called Babri Mazjid built in honour of Babar was demolished. However, the December 6, 1992, battle was not the only one waged for Ayodhya. From 1033 AD, Hindus, *Sadhus* and saints, king and warriors and the general Hindu faithful have fought seventy-nine battles for the defence of Ayodhya.

The other essential feature that was missing at the edifice at Ayodhya was the *wuzoo*, which is a slightly elevated washing place for ritual washing. Usually, the large masjids have three domes, but the two side ones are smaller than the central one. At Ayodhya, all three were of equal size. All in all, a suspicion lingered in one's mind that in all likelihood, the Babri edifice was not a masjid but actually a *dargah*, i.e., a mausoleum.

As the emphasis historically has been on the word Babri, this is another area that gives rise to suspicion. The association of an individual's name with a mosque is unusual. A masjid is a prayer hall for one and all, and is seldom named after an individual. The mosque opposite Delhi's Red Fort is called the Jama Masjid, although, figuratively speaking, it was built by Shah Jahan. The only mosque Aurangzeb was proud to have built stands at Lahore (presently in Pakistan). He called it the "Badshahi Masjid". It too, does not bear the name of a person.

Babar was busy in 1526 with the First Battle of Panipat and its aftermath. The following year, i.e., 1527 was occupied by his struggle against Maharana Sanga. He lived for only two more years and that too, in an unfamiliar foreign land, busy consolidating his Indian conquest. Nevertheless, to defeat the Hindus, he could have sent his general Mir Baqi to destroy the main temple to deliver to the Hindus of north India a humiliating message that Babar a descendant of Timur Lang, had arrived to subjugate them. To build a brand new structure replacing the earlier one would have taken a long time, plus many soldiers to guard the demolition work. One has to remember that following Babar, the short, first half of the reign of his son Humayun was shaky due to harassment by his enemies. Finally, it is unlikely that Sunnis would welcome and pray in a mosque built by a Shia like Mir Baqi. This further avers that the structure was a *dargah*. Before 1940, the litigation papers refer to the site as Masjid-e-Janmasthan.

August 5, 2020, was an epoch-making day when

Bhumi Pujan for the reconstruction of Ram Mandir at the Ramjanmabhoomi site was performed by PM Narendra Modi at Ayodhya. It marked the revival of *Bhartiya Asmita* (Indian pride) suppressed and brutalised by the Islamic invaders right from Muhammad-bin-Qasim in 712 AD which continued even after independence by chicanery of a compact between the communists, Islamists, Christian missionaries and the Nehruvian acolytes. The curriculum in the education system of India from school level to highest levels of academia was filled with a distorted history which glorified the Islamic invaders who massacred Hindus in lakhs, raped and captured Hindu women and made them sex slaves.

The wont of Islamic invaders to loot, plunder, and demolish ancient Hindu temples, totalling to more than 30,000, and building mosques or mausoleums over them has been completely denied by the leftist and Nehruvian historians. Hindus were made to feel ashamed of their own identity and past glorious achievements by constantly denigrating Vedic culture and Vedic civilisation. Brahmins were painted as vile cheats, Kshatriyas as power hungry murderous rapists and Vaishyas as conniving frauds who liked to maximise profits by duping people. Also, a fake theory of Aryan invasion was spun to instil hatred within the Vanvasis and Dalits saying that the 'upper caste' Hindus were aliens who hailed from Northern Europe and subdued the indigenous Dravidians to rule over them.

The anti-Hindu mafia also spread hatred against our revered Gods and Goddesses by disparaging Lord Ram as a misogynist who killed the benevolent ruler Ravana. Devi Kali and Durga were portrayed as very violent characters who killed Mahishasura. While this mafia tried to question the historicity of Bhagwan Ram and Krishna, they wrote paeans of praise in text books about Mohammad and Jesus Christ whose historicity is now doubted and questioned by many objective researchers.

The secular mafia indulged in this nefarious practice to keep Hindus from seeking re-possession of their holy places of worship and ancient temples converted into mosques by Islamic invaders. When devout Hindus sought re-construction of the three most holiest temples at Ayodhya, Mathura and Kashi, demolished by Islamic invaders, they were denied even that by the communists by completely falsifying history.

There are also detailed accounts of how temples were broken, gold and precious wealth was looted from them and mosques were built over them.

The Islamic structures built in a hurry by demolishing ancient temples themselves explicitly show that the intricately sculpted pillars bearing Sanskrit and various Indic inscriptions praising Vishnu, support the domes of the structures.

When Hindus petitioned the courts for possession of the holiest of sites marking the birth place of Ram, an excavation by the Archaelogical Survey of India and a Ground Penetrating Radar Survey by it found more evidence of an elaborate foundation of a Hindu religious structure beneath the mosque. Some people came with a new spin claiming that it was a Buddhist temple beneath the mosque and not a Hindu temple.

These vile arguments were countered by the Hindus and after a long and patient battle in the Courts from High Court to the Supreme Court on 9 November 2019, the Supreme Court finally awarded the Ram Janmabhoomi site to the Hindus for constructing a temple to mark Bhagwan Ram's birth place.

Notably, countless Hindus have lost their lives in their 500-year-old battle to regain the holy site from the barbarous Islamists. Every generation of Hindus since 1528 has relentlessly fought with the Islamists to regain the Ramjanmabhoomi. Even in 1990 thousands of Ram *sevaks* were brutally massacred by the UP police under the direct orders from the then UP Chief Minister, Mulayam Singh Yadav when they took out a peaceful procession for Ram Rath Yatra. Countless bodies of Hindu devotees were thrown into the river Sarayu, so much so that the waters of the Sarayu turned red with their blood.

This injustice finally led to the culmination of the demolition of the blighted mosque on December 6, 1992, which is celebrated by devout Hindus as Vijay Diwas. Of course the communists and the anti-Hindus who want to deny Hindus their fundamental right to worship at the holiest of sites, term it as a 'Black Day for Indian Democracy'.

But the same secularists are mum about the massacre, genocide and rape of Hindus in 1989-90 in Kashmir by the Islamists which also accompanied demolition of scores of temples in Jammu and Kashmir. So, it was a moral victory when Prime Minister Modi performed the *Bhumi Pujan* at the holy site marking the birth place of Bhagwan Ram for constructing a magnificent temple which would signify the eternal spirit of Sanatan Dharma as a symbol of triumph against predatory Abrahamic faiths.

We now need to put in all our efforts to liberate Krishna Janmabhoomi at Mathura and the Kashi Temple at Varanasi which were demolished by Aurangzeb in 1670 and 1669 respectively. The Krishna Janmabhoomi Mandir was originally established by Bhagwan Krishna's grandson Vajra which was rebuilt by Chandragupta II in 400 AD. It was demolished in 1017 AD by Islamic invaders. The Krishna Janmabhoomi Temple was re-built by King Bir Singh Bundela which the cruel barbaric Mughal, Aurangzeb, demolished in 1670 and built a Shahi Idgah mosque over it.

Similarly, the holy temple of Bhagwan Shiva at Kashi housing the rare *Jyotirlinga* was demolished three times by the Islamic invaders and re-built every time except the last when Aurangzeb demolished it in 1669 and built the Gyanvapi Mosque over it. It is said that the *Jyotirlinga* was saved by the priests of the holy temple from the Islamic *jihadis* and put into a well in the temple precincts. It is still lying there.

It is to be noted that the western nations, (read Christians), want us to not reclaim our ancient temples from the Islamists in the name of secular principles, but when it comes to their own interests the rule changes. For e.g., the Christians of Spain wrested back their kingdom in the sixteenth century which had been earlier invaded by the Muslim Moors in the twelfth century when the Spaniard Christians demolished all the mosques, reconverted them to churches and issued an ultimatum to Muslims residing in Spain to either leave Spain with the defeated Moors or get converted to Christianity; this diktat was implemented forcefully.

Thus, any civilisation without pride and respect for its glorious past and traditions is destined to perish unless its past glory is revived.

Renaming Nehru's House

One fails to comprehend why there is so much hullabaloo over the Nehru Museum being renamed as Prime Ministers' Museum and Library Society. In any case, it was rather incongruous, to say the least, to house Jawaharlal Nehru, then newly crowned India's Prime Minister after the British left in 1947, in the residence of the Commander-in-Chief of the British Indian Army. Nehru, of course, led with delight the taking over of the reins of power from the British Empire. However, he disliked the armed forces greatly. When General Sir MacDonald Lockhart, the British Commander-in-Chief of our army asked Prime Minister Nehru in the early days of Independence as to his broad intentions about the scope of the Indian army's missions, so that he (Lockhart) could begin planning the size and equipment of the force, Nehru's quick retort was that India believed in peace and, therefore, did not really need any army. The police that was then available in the country was adequate to protect us.

Prime Minister Nehru remained consistent in these views. He did not expand the armed forces nor did he acquire any new weaponry for them. The result was the disaster in Ladakh and N.E.F.A. (now Arunachal Pradesh). The Chinese Radio boasted that its troops looked forward to celebrating the Christmas of 1962 in Calcutta. Their invasion began on 20 October 1962 and ended with a unilateral withdrawal on the midnight of 20 and 21 November. During that unfortunate period, thousands of our army jawans laid down their lives in trying to resist the People's Liberation Army (PLA). Many more were wounded by frostbite because those soldiers who were dispatched in a hurry after the invasion began were ill-equipped. They went up the high mountains with one thin pullover, a pair of thin woollen socks and no gloves. The footwear our soldiers had was no more than ordinary canvas shoes. Thus, many unfortunate soldiers suffered frostbite.

Prime Minister Nehru was so shaken at this national humiliation that he wept on the radio while addressing the nation. His heart went out to the people of Assam, he cried in English. "Assam *khatre mein hai*", he wept in Hindi. It was a comprehensive rout presided over by General B M Kaul, who had not seen action throughout his career, and whose only qualification for being appointed army chief was that he happened to be related to Nehru. Yet, a captive establishment and fawning media shielded India's first Prime Minister from any fallout; his loud-talking and irascible, though intelligent, Defence Minister V K Krishna Menon was made the scapegoat for the 1962 disaster and was made to resign to pacify national anger.

The mother of parliaments, namely Britain's Westminster, does not provide apartments or houses to its Members of Parliament. House rent allowance is part of the basket of allowances given to the MPs. Quite contrary to what is often loudly claimed by his acolytes, democracy in our country is in no way a gift bequeathed by Nehru or his dynasty. It flourished in ancient India in myriad forms. For instance, Krishna, who is worshiped as an avatar of Lord Vishnu, was a republican himself. He was the de facto president of the Vrishni league, one among the numerous Yadava clans that made up the Confederacy of Mathura. In fact, Krishna's struggle against the rampaging Magadhan titan Jarasandha, a ruthless imperialist, was actually a struggle to protect and preserve the republican way of life against the aggrandisement of a superpower.

Democracy in India wasn't confined to Krishna and Mathura. Northwestern India had many republics that valiantly fought the invading Alexander, like the Mallas and Kshudrakas. Greek sources admit that Alexander could overcome them only after suffering considerable casualties. Vaishali, a neighbour of Magadha but at loggerheads with the latter was home to the renowned Vajji republic inhabited by the Licchavi people.

If any memorial is desired by the family or kith and kin of a deceased leader, it should be built in tune with his or her character as well as achievements. In this context, the two bungalows at Safdarjung and Akbar Road in India's capital, converted into a sort of memorial for the late Indira Gandhi is a shabby effort. One, because the bungalows were state property for ministers or officials of the state to live in; Second, the two neighbouring bungalows in no way reflect the life and work of the distinguished lady. A place at Janpath occupied by the descendants of India's second Prime Minister Lal Bahadur Shastri is another instance.

One of Jawaharlal Nehru's admirers claims that the library situated in the palatial bungalow of the former British Commander-in-Chief of the Indian Army of the colonial era has contributed a great deal to the intellectual life of the country. Now, no matter where this library might have been situated, it would have served the same purpose. In fact, architecturally, it detracts from the majesty of the Commander-in-Chief's palace. It has no memorial value, unlike the seventeenth century Mughal prince Dara Shikoh's library, which is a reminder that had he ruled India, there might have been no Partition. It has been an appropriate step taken to convert this library into a Partition Museum to enable India's present and coming generations to know what transpired in those years.

Emigration and Jihad

A point of view has been projected in the national dailies that love-*jihad*, and the societal reaction to it has become so frequent that it has become a leading cause of death among Indian youth. The net result of this fear psychosis is driving the smartest young Indians to foreign shores, and thus threatening the country's social fabric as such emigration is likely to hurt the future of the country.

In the context of India's 144 crore citizens, the incidence of love *jihad* is miniscule. Not all those who die are highly educated or particularly talented. In any case, if these few incidents can be said to be leading to large-scale emigration, the phenomenon, often looked upon as some sort of brain-drain, need not be seen as a disadvantage to the country. The émigrés of yesteryear can also be seen as our ambassadors of today. The more the number of non-resident Indians (NRIs) the bigger the advantage; they are also a source of influence for India abroad. Right through history, India has not had an imperialistic or colonising mindset. Yet, influence overseas is important, more so as the world is proceeding towards becoming a united whole.

Was it not good to see our Prime Minister being sought after by the American President, seeking the vote of Indian immigrants who have become citizens of the United States of America? In case we are apprehensive of a brain drain, preventing or discouraging emigration is hardly the step to resort to. We have a population huge enough to be able to absorb emigration of any size. What we do not have in adequacy are the educational facilities, in quantity as well as quality to educate and train the young population. In fact, in the basket of education, we should include the teaching of foreign languages. For example, it is believed that at the current rate of decline in population, there would be no Japan left in another hundred years. Our aspiring youth should consider learning how to live and flourish in Japan. As far as population goes, Russia has already fallen to becoming a country smaller than Pakistan.

Coming back to the subject of love *jihad*, has anyone asked why no one has protested against a "love crusade?" Christianity, like Islam, is also a religion of the book. From a bride's point of view, a Christian male can have only one wife. If he wishes to divorce her, the challenge before him would be like that facing any other husband. For a Roman Catholic, the Church does not permit a divorce under any circumstances. In any case, the fundamental Christian ethic is that marriage is a sacrament, divine and indivisible.

In Islam, marriage is a contract, which can be cancelled by divorce, by the husband giving the wife three notices of '*talaq*' spread over three months even if verbally. Moreover, even without resorting to divorce, the husband can take on three more wives at a time. If the reader were a parent of daughters, would they prefer a 'love-*jihad* or love-crusade?'

I recently came across a book *The Long Divergence: How*

Islamic Laws Held Back the Middle East by Prof Timur Kuran, who is a Turkish scholar teaching at the Duke University, USA. In the course of his lengthy presentation, he has pointed out several laws that have held back the progress of West Asia for centuries. It is only petroleum that has brought prosperity for as long as demand lasts or the wells dry up.

While discussing the views of Prof Kuran with (the late) Dr Yoginder Alagh, who had been a vice-chancellor of the Jawaharlal Nehru University (JNU) as well as a minister in the Deve Gowda, and Inder Gujral regimes at the centre during 1996-98, some interesting points were discussed. That the Green Revolution logically should have taken place first in the UP-Bihar-Bengal belt because the waters of the Ganga and Yamuna flow through these states. UP has begun progressing recently, whereas Bihar and West Bengal have yet to follow. Prof Alagh attributed this phenomenon to the socio-communal profile of the people, an opinion that may understandably cause disquiet to many, but one that would be hard to dismiss, statistically and objectively speaking.

The discussion at hand merits a more dispassionate analysis than the usual hand-wringing and often one-sided blame game one is accustomed to seeing. It is true that there have been incidents wherein members of the majority community have felt outraged enough to take the law into their own hands to settle what is perceived as a deliberate slight to their sentiments and even way of life. Also, incidents where the womenfolk of only a particular section are targeted for fraudulent marriages that usually have ulterior motives, namely, religious conversions, have only added fuel to the fire of an already inflamed polity. With past administrations either turning a blind eye to repeated offences by one community, either in a bid to appear secular or more acutely, to perpetuate their hold over votebanks, this problem had already assumed a gargantuan nature. That many among the majority have become emboldened now to resort to lesser subtle methods of reclaiming their identity merits an honest look, and not a diatribe based on worn out shibboleths.

India's Diplomacy Needs Reform

A reform of India's diplomatic network is much needed. As far as is publicly known, foreign policy has been handled much better in the few years than ever before. The diplomatic network, however, is in need of up-gradation.

The nations our foreign policy and establishment engages with need to be divided into three categories. Those requiring a continual contact, political as well as economic, would be about ten or twelve, in which the US, Russia, China, the UK, France, Germany, Japan, Israel, Saudi Arabia and Australia, possibly Brazil too, would figure. These may be designated as category 'X' countries. Then there would be many countries that commercially have a lot of potential. For the moment though, these might require only occasional political or diplomatic attention like say, Taiwan, Vietnam, Mongolia, Spain, Argentina, Egypt, and some countries in Africa. The interaction with these countries would have significant commercial potential, which would also include tourist inflow from these countries. They may, therefore, be categorised as belonging to 'Group A'. The rest of the countries, small or medium-sized could be categorised under 'Group B'.

There could be a category 'C' that would include those countries with whom India presently does not have any significant diplomatic contact, but which in the foreseeable future could turn important. While no immediate name comes to mind, countries like Moldova in Eastern Europe or a few in Africa could be cases in point. In the coming years, India should avoid being out of contact with any country. The Indian diaspora in this context should be useful to represent New Delhi on an honorary basis.

Indian representatives in category 'C' countries must be in telephonic contact with their counterparts in the neighbouring countries.

The 'X' category countries could continue to be run as hitherto, with reinforcement with an officer familiar with exports, imports as well as tourism. It hardly needs to be emphasised that tourism is one sure way of earning foreign exchange. The government hardly needs to make any capital expenditure here. The sights to be seen by the foreign visitors are aplenty; for example, the Taj Mahal at Agra or the Ajanta and Ellora Caves in Maharashtra are already there. The expenditure on infrastructural improvement would be financed mostly by the private sector. What is needed to be done by the government is mostly promotion of the heritage and attractions, as well of the facilities, but the marketing function should ideally be handled by the respective marketing divisions of the embassies. Similarly, this division should remain in touch with the exports and imports of the country concerned as well as the local conventions and peculiarities of the country concerned. These would be a guide to aspiring traders from India. Information with regard to the local traders keen to deal with India could be a useful guide for those in India who would be keen to exploit or import.

This evidently implies that new entrants to the country's foreign service should pick up sufficient working knowledge of international trade and local conditions before they plunge into responsible work. Such officials would be better suited to head Indian missions in category 'A' countries as distinct from categories 'B' or 'C'. They need not be super-experts on international affairs, which is highly essential for the 'X' category countries.

We then come to the level of category 'B' countries, which need diplomats only at the level of charge d'affaires. But they should be in contact with senior ambassadors in the region, to report as well as obtain guidance. In short, our aim should be to remain in touch with the goings-on in nearly all countries in the world, especially with a view to not miss out on commercial opportunities, however apparently small. The small countries, let us say in Group 'C', could have local citizens friendly with the Indian embassy or establishment, and they could be appointed as honorary envoys who would bear all the local costs.

Many earnest well to-to-do individuals may be attracted to such appointments for the sake of local status, as well as the few privileges a diplomat would enjoy. It is likely that such envoys would be better informed about local developments than the conventional diplomatic representatives, who in any case, would cost the country's exchequer quite a bit. Also, such informal appointees would know the local language(s) spontaneously.

My own experience has been that it is difficult to understand a person's mentality fully, unless one knows his or her language. How many languages can a professional career diplomat learn? Not many. It is therefore, food for thought whether every embassy should have an honorary member diplomat who is a local. However, it bears iteration here that knowledge of the languages on non-English speaking countries in category 'X' countries is a must, in order to accurately understand the milieu of those countries, and to be able to gauge the ongoing developments and potential changes likely to happen in those countries, which are bound to cast a profound impact on India. Lack of such linguistic proficiency in the country's diplomatic core has cost us in the past.

Ghulam Nabi Indicates a Churn

Recently, former Congressman Ghulam Nabi Azad stated publicly that six hundred years ago there were no Muslims in Kashmir. This is well known, but that a distinguished politician should say this is historic. Is this a symptom of loss of confidence that the above-mentioned leader's community has suffered with the march of time? Contrast this statement with Jinnah's speech of March 22, 1940, preparatory to the Pakistan Resolution passed the next day. On that occasion, he stated rather bluntly, but unambiguously, that Hindus and Muslims could not live together in the same country. They are two different people with not only different but mutually antagonistic views of life, he had said.

As if this was not enough, a few weeks ago Afghanistan's Taliban rulers even more bluntly said that "The idea of Pakistan is dead". The Balochs, Pakhtoons and Sindhis are now out on the streets, openly demanding independence from the New Medina, whose dream was sold to them in 1947. Pakhtoons and Balochs have gone so far as to threaten Pakistan, "The Bengalis (i.e., East Pakistanis) took off your pants (in 1971), but we Pakhtoons and Balochs will skin you this time".

Over these eighty-four years, the subcontinent of India has turned a full 180 degrees. Evidently, the secession of Bangladesh from Pakistan was the first blow. It proved that their religion could not hold a country together. The theory spun by Jinnah had been shown to be hollow. If the theory perpetuates itself, it would contain the portents of further disintegration. Pakistan, which had come into being as a dream of a New Medina, suffered a shattering loss of prestige. With it, the image of the country in the world was also shaken. The next setback was Pakistan's defeat in the Kargil War of 1999. Its humiliating withdrawal from Indian territory further eroded whatever military prestige it had left.

A very unexpected development, in due course was, the coming of Narendra Modi to power at the Centre. Initially, it was not expected to be a very different phenomenon from what had been seen earlier, and Pakistan as well as its terrorist proxies in the Kashmir Valley continued with their infiltration and violent attacks. The suicide bombing of Indian soldiers at Pulwama was particularly brutal. However, this time, Pakistan was forced to pay a prohibitive price by New Delhi's retaliation in the form of the Indian Air Force's bombing of Pakistani terror camps at Balakot. The Indian retribution shook Pakistan and its sympathisers as never before.

The next blow was the abrogation of Article 370, which, for all practical purposes, drove virtually the last nail in the coffin of the so-called Kashmir dispute. Pakistan has apparently fallen in line with the reality that it is no use raising the issue anymore. Moreover, some leaders in Pak-occupied Kashmir (PoK) have begun to claim that they belong to India because as per the Indian Independence Act of 1947 passed by the British

Parliament, the (erstwhile) Maharaja of Jammu & Kashmir had acceded to the Indian Union.

Even more than the Balakot strike, what has hurt Pakistan is demonetisation, carried out by the Modi government in 2016. Previously, Pakistani as well as Indian currency notes were supplied by the same printer in Britain, giving Islamabad free access to Indian currency. The change of currency was a huge economic setback to the Pak economy. Eventually, this has led to virtual bankruptcy in that country. The impression in India is that the middle and lower classes across the border are mostly subsisting on a single meal a day. The American dollar is valued at over 300 Pakistani rupees which have lost any meaningful value. Internationally, the destruction of the twin towers of the World Trade Centre in New York on 9/11 has generated a great deal of prejudice. Terrorism in general has certainly not added goodwill. To add to all this, of course, are the pressures brought upon by modernisation, particularly the revolution let loose by Information Technology on a community that is essentially conservative but also orthodox.

In the light of these developments, Ghulam Nabi Azad's statement about Islam being no older than 1,400 years in the Kashmir Valley may well be pregnant with vision. It may be calling for a revolution in the thinking of the community's clergy. For example, its attitude towards the advent of a uniform civil code. While the legal and constitutional journey towards this goal will be a saga by itself, what is pertinent is that many Muslim women have begun speaking up against the practice of instant *talaq* (divorce), and in favour of their rights as citizens governed by an egalitarian constitutional framework. Added to this, there is a small but growing community of people who are no longer afraid to call themselves "Ex-Muslim"; the nomenclature is self-explanatory.

But while the churn in the community merits our attention and study, its attendant turmoil in the neighbourhood must immediately occupy the attention of our rulers and policymakers, as a breakdown there has all the potential of adversely affecting India's rise.

True Federalism

India often claims to be a pluralistic society and proudly proclaims that it is unity in diversity. No doubt, Hindu faith provides us with a strong shaft to hold the country together. Nevertheless, there is an occasional deviation in our dealing with some of our linguistic brethren. They show up prominently at election time.

West Bengal is dominantly a Hindu state like any other; but it is what may be called a state of *shakta* worshipping people. Male deities are not sought after. Although Krishna is acceptable, yet more by the lower castes who were attracted to Chaitanya Mahaprabhu. Otherwise, the popular deities are Durga and Mahakali; more the latter. This translates into domestic life with a father often addressing his daughter affectionately as Maa. Even a lady is to be addressed respectfully. Didi is the next best to Maa. Another unusual practice to be witnessed at a wedding reception called popularly *bohubhat*, a party given by the groom's family after the wedding. The odd lady might well instinctively remark 'how handsome is the groom?' Across India it is the bride whose looks are commented upon, not the groom's, but here is where West Bengal is different. The Bengali super-performance is their language; neither religion, nor the culture. A non-Bengali speaking it as well as a native would touch their hearts. If the language is spoken well by an outsider, it would be appreciated as '*parishkar*' (clear). An even better performance would evoke the compliment of '*sundar*' (beautiful).

In sharp contrast, Gujarat or Rajasthan would not be as sensitive as Bengal over the issue of language. The Tamilian is flattered if an outsider speaks the language authentically. It is likely to be taken as an outsider having taken all the trouble to identify himself culturally with their ancient land and culture.

To the Maharashtrian, his Marathi language is very important. For example, in the composite Bombay State, the Maharashtrians were in an overwhelming majority and yet they agitated—with and without violence—to get a *Samyukta* Maharashtra, distinct from Gujarat, which was the other component of the state. It is not that they disliked the Gujaratis; there are millions of them in Mumbai, and the two communities co-exist happily. But they had to have a separate Marathi-speaking state to be proud of.

All in all, every community, whether linguistic or otherwise, is likely to be proud of its identify. At least for those who wish to get elected and govern, they should take it for granted that identify is important to most and should be prepared to appear to pamper them. The reason is that in the event some adverse incident takes place, it could well become an issue of identity, whose flames would then be difficult to douse. By and large, India has managed its many languages and pluralities competently.

However, with the rapidly developing economy and the resultant prosperity expected in due course, one cannot rule out the desire for relative freedom, and the demand for greater regional authority. The current government has been wise not to touch Article 356 of the Constitution and dismiss any state government, an act that is viewed as an anti-federal action. Other factors have also helped, such as the presence of minorities, who often wave the flag of polarisation, in turn, leaving no choice for the majority other than a strident march towards unity. UP, which was the torch-bearer for Hindi, remained comparatively dormant, as its problems for decades were economic rather than political. Another factor that worked in India's favour was the awareness that Pakistan split into two in 1971 merely on the issue of its national language Urdu. Much later, the traumatic breakup of the Soviet Union into sixteen republics sent waves of fear through many countries. More secession followed in Europe after 1991. There is no danger of this happening on the horizon of India at present.

In today's world of increasing technology, a small state is a handicapped polity. Even in older times, the defence of a small state was perpetually problematic. There are a few such states in India's neighbourhood and we can appreciate their tensions. In the event there comes a phase of financial shortage, borrowing would pose a problem. What and how much can a small state pledge as collateral security?

The problem of defence can be answered by joining an alliance. A number of European countries have linked themselves to the North Atlantic Treaty Organisation (NATO). But there is a price to pay for an alliance. One's freedom to conduct one's foreign policy shrinks simultaneously. It gets yoked to the essential pre-requisites of the major alliance partner.

Even larger states must ensure that they are well armed, not only for themselves but also for friendly nations. For example, go back to the 1860s and the American Civil War when the northern and southern states fought for years. If the USA had not remained together and united, there would have been no country to save Europe from the Nazis in WWII, and also WWI between 1914-18.

National political parties should, therefore, have units of young people, men and women, who can keep track of regional peculiarities and systematically learn and practise them so that communication with the regions becomes more effective.

The Opposition is Incompetent

Since 2014, not once has the Centre used Article 356 of the Constitution to dismiss state governments. During the previous 63 years, Article 356 was used 120 times.

The Emergency of June 1975 lasted till the general elections in early 1977. During that year and a half, there was order without law in the country. That isn't so now and yet the Opposition keeps saying that "democracy in India is in danger".

The Emergency was imposed mainly in the Hindi-speaking states, with forced sterilisation of men. The main targets were Muslim and Muslim youth; three mothers we met had their sons away into the fields well before dawn every day not to return until nightfall, so that they could be safe from *nasbandi*.

The real problem has been the Opposition and that too since the time we got independence. Most times, it has been weak, divided and untrained in governance. The communist parties have retained their Marxist ideologies, quite oblivious that these ideologies perished as long ago as 1991. There is hardly any other political party that has a coherent ideology. A few of them, like the Akali Dal for example, have programmes, which is to retain its control over Sikh institutions. Tamil Nadu's DMK has hung on to its anti-Brahminism; the rest function according to opportunistic causes that come their way. The members of all such parties are more beholden to the street than the assembly halls of legislatures.

Most Indian politicians may have never heard of the concept of a shadow cabinet, which is very useful to the opposition party, so that at least some members of the party have a working knowledge of subjects like foreign affairs, finance, defence etc. This would make it easy for the Opposition to oppose the government and not let it get away with an incorrect or inadequate policy. After an election, if the Opposition is able to participate in the formation of a cabinet in a new government, it would have several readymade ministers who would be well versed in their respective subjects.

This decline began soon after Jawaharlal Nehru's death. One of the Prime Ministers who came after him declared, "Corruption is a global phenomenon and it is difficult to name a country that is free of corruption". These utterances turned out to be a signal to India's politicians that politics can be a lucrative business. Come election time, a party begins by selling the application forms of party tickets to candidates. Thereafter, when the party is ready to distribute the tickets, each ticket attracts good money. The entire election expense is to be met by the candidate. Win or lose, at the end of the election, every party can hope to make a tidy profit.

As the lure of money shone more and more, the significance of talent, popularity and political competence began to diminish and gradually disappear. The other consequence of increasing wealth led to parental compulsions of bequeathing one's political party to one's son or daughter. That is how dynastic politics began and has today engulfed many a party, kicking the issue of talent to a distant background. Is it not a shame that such a large country as ours should have to make do with only one national party at a time? For long years, the Congress was the only national party. There was no alternative that could replace it in the event of its losing power. Three or four coalition governments did manage to keep the country going; one government had as many as 24 parties. How can the country expect to progress, and that too speedily, with "Common Minimum Programmes?" If there is serious disagreement among the parties, would the country's integrity be assured? How would other countries view such a coalition-ruled nation? How tied down the Prime Minister of such a coalition would be, merely to keep the coalition partners satisfied?

The Bharatiya Janata Party (BJP) or its precursor the Bharatiya Jana Sangh (BJS) took sixty-two years to come to power. Nevertheless, it was a blessing that it rose to the occasion when the Congress reached a state of decline. The speedy rise of the country in the world in the last few years should open our eyes to a universal weakness of democratic politics. Almost all political ideologies are unconnected with the ethos of the countries that adhere to them, or claim to do so. They are based on academic theories and less in the soil of the countries practising them. We have seen conservative parties, liberal platforms, socialist organisations, communist groups, fascist movement *et al.* Not a single one of these has been born of the soil of any country.

The BJP has demonstrated how speedily the people can respond to Hindu nationalism rather than to a socialistic pattern of society, which is alien. The only example of such rapidity of response was the Muslim League, which won Partition in a mere seven years' time. This again, can be called an ethnic response. Can Indian democracy throw up ethnic alternatives? It seems difficult if not doubtful.

How to Allot Lok Sabha Seats in 2026

After general elections in independent India began in 1952, a revision of the number of Lok Sabha seats became due in the year 1973. It was then decided by the Central cabinet that the revision should be postponed and the problem be looked at again in due course in 2026. The reason was that in the early decades of independence, there was an uneven growth in the population of India's states. As a result, those states that did not take family planning seriously due to the higher growth rate of their respective populations would have to be allotted more seats than hitherto. For example, UP, Bihar and Rajasthan would get more seats than Punjab and the conscientious states of South India, whose populations were controlled thanks to family planning being adopted more seriously. Some southern MPs argued that states which had practised family planning effectively were getting a lesser increase in MPs than states which had not done so. They argued that in order to prevent changes in the balance of power in favour of laggard states, the number of seats in Lok Sabha should be frozen at the existing levels. The Delimitation Commission recommended freezing the number of Lok Sabha seats at the 1971 level after which the Government of India could decide on de-freezing the number of seats and increasing them.

The country certainly needed disciplined family planning as it could not have borne the consequences of an unbridled population growth without a check. Regardless, in 2023, we have overtaken China as the world's largest country in terms of population. It is indeed true that population can also yield dividends by providing the country with more and more working young people to support their older compatriots who will work and produce less. Countries aspiring to grow and retain their growth cannot do without a large working population. Japan is an example; if the land of the rising sun continues to trundle along at its present birth rate, its entire society may go out of existence in the course of a century.

Japan's opposite in this regard is India. The question is: can our country's educational facilities keep pace with this expanding torrent of births? We would need a phenomenal growth in the number of educational institutions from primary schools to colleges and universities, and, needless to add, of a competitive quality. An uneducated population would be a big burden on the economy, more so in a technologically advancing world. India can provide excellent education, but nowhere near the level of reaching every aspirant. The country needs technocrats, entrepreneurs and managers; certainly not more of class IV labour, beggars and vagabonds.

Keeping most factors in view, before the year 2026 arrives, our Election Commission should keep track of the GDP of every state separately, as well as its per capita over five years. After all, the increased number of human heads in a state should not entitle it to obtain more Lok Sabha seats in 2026. In fact, the present Central government's priority is economic growth. Prime Minister Narendra Modi often says that we want to become the world's third largest economy and thereafter, aspire to be the world's second largest. Unless the states also perform in the global race of economic growth, how can the country as a whole compete successfully? It is, therefore, more than advisable to include the state GDP as well as the GDP of the state per capita (i.e., individual GDP) of each state separately in this calculus of fresh allotment of seats to the Parliament and later to legislatures as well.

Literacy, both male and female—but calculated separately—should also be a criterion for the number of Lok Sabha seats to be allotted to each state. After all, literacy is an important aspect of development and progress. The gender ratio of the number of females per 100 males should also be a qualification, while allotting seats. We have come a long way towards equalising this ratio, especially since the Prime Minister has proclaimed *Beti Bachao, Beti Padhao* as a national mission. The more equal the ratio, the greater the advantage ought to accrue to states when it comes to deciding on allocating new Lok Sabha seats.

The health standards of the state, which include not only the measure of how well the citizenry is keeping, but also the number of healthcare facilities and health services, ought to be a deciding factor in this regard. As a Nobel Laureate put it, health plus education means socioeconomic progress. One must also lay stress on women and children's health as criteria that must be mandatorily taken into account while awarding increased legislative seats to states. To avoid doubts and controversy, the Election Commission might consider an international body like the World Health Organisation (WHO) to certify which state is performing well or otherwise on these parameters and how and why?

The Election Commission would know the nuances of this problem, and may well be able to think of other criteria but many would certainly agree that allotting Lok Sabha seats by counting heads would be the most primitive method and would naturally arouse untold controversy.

The Dance of History

On the Basant Panchami of the year 2024, on the desert plane of Abu Dhabi, history performed what can arguably be called its first dance in the realm of faith, religion and God. Never before has Islam shaken hands with the idol-worshipping Hindus. The religion of Prophet Mohammad has accepted the Jews and Christians as *Ahl-e-Qitab*, meaning, People of the Book, whether of the Torah or Bible. Muslims have also obeyed and strictly adhered to the third of Prophet Moses' Commandments: "Thee shall not make any gravel image of thy Lord the God".

That is why idols or statues of any kind were abandoned by all three religions originating from the credo of Prophet Moses, whose inspiration Prophet Moses followed up. No act by their followers to even attempt to have a glimpse of God can ever be countenanced by these faiths. The synagogue, church and mosque have been limited to being only prayer halls, unlike the Hindu temple, which is looked upon as a residence of the divine. Ramakrishna Paramahansa, Swami Vivekananda and Maharshi Aurobindo, for example, confessed to having seen the divine. Until now, this has been a fundamental difference between the Hindu and Abrahamic faiths; the latter have preferred to destroy idols rather than allow them to distract the devotion of their adherents. This fundamental gulf of faith explains the catalogue of iconoclasms that litter Indian medieval history.

That is why it appears incredible to believe that any human being can achieve two victories in the course of only two years—the first at Ayodhya and the other now at Abu Dhabi. Ayodhya represents the correction of history of iconoclasm while the event at Abu Dhabi reveals the nobility of King Zayed, the monarch of the United Arab Emirates (UAE), in wiping off some of the tears dripping from Hindu eyes, who, over the course of a millennium, lost thousands of their temples to iconoclasm.

King Zayed has shown the courage that perhaps no monarch in history has. There have been many kings who have made history, have invented systems and legislated path-breaking laws. It is, however, difficult to think of a monarch who has reversed history and turned his back on the past with such ease. For a thousand years now, Islam has chosen the path of orthodoxy—minimal change—and has done its best to avoid reinterpretation—embracing new ways when necessary. The objective was to conserve the strength and unity of Islam and not allow it to dissipate.

When it came to numbers, therefore, Islam has been an expanding torrent. What King Zayed has done is to pick up a hitherto untouchable aspect, reinterpretation, and in doing so has touched the hearts of 140 crore Indians. How many Muslim hearts might have been irritated by this remains to be seen. But the notes emanating from this seminal event are likely to be less than pleasant to a lot of ears around the Islamic world. Pockets are easier to open; hearts are far more difficult to persuade, which is what King Zayed has done. He can, however, be sure that most

Hindus will pray for his happiness as long as history is written.

The opening of the grand Hindu temple in Abu Dhabi also has the potential to trigger off schisms in the Abrahamic faith world, particularly Islam. However, this need not necessarily be an unwelcome development. Not only will millions of Hindus flock there, their inflow will also bring in billions of dollars as revenue from tourism and the businesses that flow from it. The Muslim world, which has been negligent towards commerce, will have a chance to rectify this lacuna. This marvel of sculpture, which is also a live and functioning museum of the most exquisite carvings consecrated by the confluence of the holy waters of the Ganga, Yamuna and Saraswati specially brought from India is precisely the edifice, platform and opportunity for that.

Prime Minister Modi's inauguration and worship at this sprawling and breathtaking Hindu temple is in a sense, not only the rise of Sanatana Dharma in the desert, but also a reversal of centuries of crusades and Ghaznavism. The temple, which of course has the icons of deities, is also rich with carvings, sculpted images and bass reliefs, including those of animals and birds; one could also liken it to a veritable museum-cum-zoo of stone. Modi is a practising and worshipping Hindu, something that comes through clearly, whether at Kathmandu, Varanasi, Ayodhya, Rameshwaram or Abu Dhabi. Bhakti is visible and convincing only when it emanates from the heart; otherwise, it is nothing but the enactment of a ritual without devotion.

Obama, Muslims and India

When Dr Manmohan Singh was Prime Minister, he repeatedly declared "Muslims First", "15 per cent of the country's resources should be earmarked for the Muslims", etc. For some leaders around the world, this has become the starting point of understanding India. Evidently, former US President Barack Obama has been one of those individuals who picked up this delusional understanding of India. Nonetheless, it seems to have crystallised into his opinion of what India was.

Barouk or Barack was the horse that carried the Holy Prophet to heaven from Jerusalem and also brought him back. Husein was the brother of al Hasan, the Prophet's grandson who was in line to become the fifth Caliph. These holy names were given to Obama though his mother had him baptised in a church. A special corner of his heart naturally beats for the denizens of the *ummah*.

After Pakistan's breakup in 1971, Obama seemed concerned that India too should not "fall apart", in his own terminology. He might not be aware that India was partitioned in 1947; he was not born then. In fact, most people today would be unfamiliar with the history of how Pakistan and Bangladesh have treated the Hindus; from previously being one-third of the population in 1947 they have been reduced to minuscule percentages through persecution, ethnic cleansing and expulsion.

Pakistan's founder Mohammad Ali Jinnah and his senior colleagues wanted an exchange of populations on the lines of what had taken place between the Christians and Muslims of Greece and Turkey respectively, under the auspices of the League of Nations, the predecessor of today's United Nations Organisation (UNO). But India's then political leaders rejected this proposal, as a result of which India today has some 18 per cent Muslims in its total population.

Islamic countries, for example Turkey, could hardly believe that these Indian leaders could be so gullible. The great sociologist Joseph Ernest Renan believed that a nation's total soul had to be one for it to be happy and remain united. In fact, the phenomenon to be compared with is the Hindu belief that the Divine or the *Paramatma* is the total soul of all living beings. Those whose individual souls are not in tune with the rest of the nation are detached from this nationhood, no matter where they reside. Religion is not crucial to the sense of the nation; what matters is one's attitude.

Had Obama's soul been wholly in tune with the universe, his utterance would not have occurred just when his entire country was celebrating a hugely successful visit by India's Prime Minister. He would have also worried about the minorities in Pakistan, and Bangladesh. The former American President's utterances only irritated the majority in India and possibly harmed the minority interests. The world at large could not care less.

Pakistan's founder Mohammad Ali Jinnah had said:

> The problem in India is not that of an inter-communal character but manifestly of an international one, and must be treated as such. So long as this basic and fundamental truth is not realised, any constitution that may be built will result in disaster and will prove destructive and harmful not only to the Muslims but also to the British and Hindus. It is a dream that the Hindus and Muslims can ever evolve a common nationality. This notion of one Indian nation has gone far beyond the limits and is the cause of most of our troubles and will lead India to destruction if we fail to revise this misconception in time. The Hindus and Muslims have different religious philosophies, social customs and literatures. They neither intermarry nor interdine and, indeed, they belong to two different civilisations which are based mainly on conflicting ideas and conceptions. Their views of life are different. It is also quite clear that Hindus and Muslims derive their inspiration from different sources of history. They have different epics, and different heroes in different episodes. To yoke together two such nations under a single state, one a numerical minority and the other a majority, must lead to growing discontent and the final destruction of any fabric that may be so built up for the government of such a state.

The Partition of India made Hindus believe that Pakistan was for Muslims and Hindustan was for Hindus and others. When they woke up after Partition they were surprised to see the Muslims largely where they were, whereas new Hindus had arrived in hundreds of thousands. Over the decades, people forgot this historical experience. Why on earth was Obama trying to open these wounds all over again?

From the USA, Prime Minister Narendra Modi visited Egypt. There, the grand mufti of Cairo as well as the Indian Bohra Muslim community resident in Egypt tried to do the opposite, though there was very little time to do so. Sadly, Barack Obama, despite his elevation to the world's highest political office of the world's leading nation, showed himself to be unequal to the responsibility of rising up to genuine global statesmanship.

Civilisation and the UCC

In the public discussions that have been sparked off recently, the overwhelming emphasis of the speakers and writers is mostly on the politics of the Uniform Civil Code (UCC). Upon which vote bank will the UCC have the maximum effect and which section is likely to oppose it and why, seems to be the thrust of most arguments. However, we have yet to see a contention based on India's historical or civilisational perspective. In terms of history, there was very little progress. Since Islamic invasions began with the appearance of Mohammad bin Qasim in 712 AD and on a large scale with Mahmud of Ghazni, civilisationally, it was as if largely the Indian society became benumbed. It is true that the regional languages and the Bhakti movements began to flourish in the medieval period. The basic reason must have been that the alien culture or way of life threw the indigenous civilisation off balance, preventing it from continuing to tick and thrive. The primary anxiety of people and their rulers would have been to look out for when and from where the next invasion was coming. American philosopher and historian Will Durant had said about the Islamic invasions of India: "The

Muslim conquest of India is the bloodiest story in history. It is a discouraging tale, for its moral is that the complex order of civilisation may at any time be overthrown by barbarians invading from without or multiplying within".

In this context, it is important to remember Dr B R Ambedkar. He had said that he would not like to die a Hindu, but he rejected both Christianity and Islam as alternatives to convert to. The reason he gave was that these were alien religions and not even remotely indigenous. They would, therefore, distance his people from the land of their birth. In the end, Babasaheb chose Buddhism as the religion to convert to.

All that we have said does not mean that we see this as India's chance to impose Indian values upon other's religious affairs, or that it is desirable to do so. The generation that framed Article 44, which says, "The state shall endeavour to secure for the citizens a Uniform Civil Code throughout the territory of India", was probably more liberal than its counterparts today. Also, more bloodshed and rioting took place then than today. The Partition had just taken place and Prime Minister Jawaharlal Nehru's thoughts were farthest from causing any hurt to minority sentiments. Yet, Article 44 was framed and included in the Constitution to ensure that this important measure of the Uniform Civil Code was not forgotten.

The Hindu Code Bill, 1955, was a further reminder that personal laws need reform. The late Syed Shahbuddin, a diplomat-turned-politician, told me years ago that he had persuaded the then Prime Minister Rajiv Gandhi to overturn the Supreme Court judgement, whereby the old Muslim lady, Shah Bano was granted a small alimony as required by the Indian Penal Civil Code. Shahbuddin's argument was that the Muslim Women's Act, 1986 would become the precedent for the Muslim clergy to accept Parliament's intervention in their (Muslim clerics') domain and affairs. I could not make out whether the Syed was serious or jesting with me, but he did seem rather proud of this achievement of his.

All in all, the thrust of our submission is that a country flourishes only if it is able to depend on its own genius. Can we not see the difference between the snail's pace of our journey as a nation since Independence and the speed with which India has galloped after the year 2014? This is so, because its indigenous way of life is getting a free hand. The more uniform our laws and procedures are, the faster we can move, unhindered by contradictions and differences.

One may look at Europe today. The two World Wars did immense damage to the continent; even then, it is difficult to imagine Europe without communism, socialism and wasteful welfarism. How much stronger could the countries of Europe have been without these ideologies is indeed a moot point.

What began with Karl Marx was essentially a movement of anti-production obsessed with distribution. With no owner overseeing any productive asset, corruption was inevitable. That this was an unwanted and definitively harmful intervention was proved by the demise of the Soviet economy and the Soviet Union itself, and every other communist economy for that matter. What is toxic about communism is probably half as damaging about socialism. Every nation competing with every other was the secret behind European success.

German Polymath Oswald Spengler, in his *The Decline of the West* (published in two volumes during 1918-22) sounded a serious note of pessimism for Western civilisation as early as a century ago. In his analysis he put forth the idea that cultures imprint upon mankind their own form, their own ideas, and passions (Spengler called this historical relativism). Each one, like a plant, goes through the appointed course of youth, maturity, and decline, a process he described as determinism.

The formation and furtherance of the European Union has undercut the secret of European success. Nor has unbridled immigration from weak and damaged economies, mostly from the Third World, lent any strength or advantage to Europe. On the one hand, the West has pursued welfarism in its factories and industries, and on the other, they have welcomed immigrant labour. These are the ways in which many a European country has lost its way. It is still not too late to make a correction by going back to European strengths and keep away from unwanted alien weaknesses.

For India, the year 2014 marks the beginning of a new era. If it does not stick to the rational path it has now taken, it would return to its slow, slothful and self-destructive ways. The presence of two laws in one country, sooner or later begins to undercut its very existence. That is the importance of the Uniform Civil Code in the larger context. Civilisations and cultures are great things, but one cannot ignore the cold fact that they are at the end of the day, a numbers' game. No matter how great a civilisation is, if it does not have adequate numbers of people who believe in and adhere to it and are willing to stand up for it, it will become an endangered species sooner or later.

International Politics

China's Belligerence Masks Its Anxiety

China's failure to intervene during the visit of Nancy Pelosi, (former Speaker of the US House of Representatives), to Taiwan, notwithstanding the threats dished out by the Communist regime, including President Xi Jinping, is a serious diplomatic setback for the country. Beijing's failure to act despite its dire threats—and this included threatening to shoot down the aircraft carrying Pelosi—is easy to understand but difficult for the Communist regime to explain. Evidently, the Chinese leadership is not mature enough to play on the world stage, leave alone be any sort of world leader.

India and its politicians till recently had been treating the Chinese with far more deference than they deserve. The last war the People's Liberation Army (PLA), as the army in China is called, fought was against Vietnam in 1979, in which it was roundly defeated and chased out of Vietnamese territory. Thereafter, for more than forty-four years, the PLA has been untested on the battlefront. On the other hand, the Indian Army has participated in many an encounter in different terrains. Unfortunately, the memories of the 1962 humiliation continued to have disproportionate influence on the Indian psyche all these years.

The PLA belongs to the Communist Party of China (CPC). Its soldiers serve the party and not the country or its citizens. A soldier can give up his blood in a spirit of patriotism, but to sacrifice his life to please his employer, in this case the party, is a difficult if not impossible proposition. In the early days of the Communist revolution, the men under arms might have been inclined to see class revolution as a cause, but such an outlook cannot be indefinite. This perhaps explains why the party did not expose its army on the battlefield. While India lost in the 1962 border war with China, the same Indian Army however, only five years later in 1967, performed admirably against the same enemy in 1967, forcibly throwing out the invading Chinese army at Nathu La. The Nathu La Pass today is India's territory. The critical element was leadership.

We should be focusing on the internal goings-on in China. Noted American columnist and analyst, Gordon Chang, tells us that China's economy grew by 0.4 per cent in the second quarter of 2022. This particular statistic comes from China's National Bureau of Statistics. However, according to many independent observers and commentators, China's economy has not only contracted but is also in a free fall. While the Chinese Communist Party claimed that trade will lift China towards its goal of around 5.5 per cent growth for the year 2022, as announced earlier the actual growth is on a downward trend. This year's first quarter showed only a 4.8 per cent growth, again China's official statistics.

The country has also seen massive protests over the decision by Chinese authorities to freeze the deposits of banks based in rural areas. The largest such demonstration by depositors demanding their lifetime savings, in Zhengzhou city in the country's Henan province, was violently crushed by the police. Runs on Chinese banks have become more frequent in recent years. Many banks have ben accused of financial improprieties and corruption. CNN estimates that as many as four lakh customers across China were unable to access their savings in rural banks in the Henan and Anhui provinces. But these are manifestations on the surface of a much bigger problem.

Its decades of rapid growth, thanks to a single party dictatorship, has enabled China to reach the position of the world's second largest economy (measured by purchasing power parity). Chinese investments are spread across the globe, and Beijing is pushing hard for obtaining influence in the Asian and African theatre by dangling the carrot of lucrative projects. Some of these countries indeed have fallen for China's ready-currency-no-questions-asked diplomacy, only to rue their haste later, as they have been enmeshed in China's debt trap. Chinese leaders are dreaming some very big dreams. They want to absorb Taiwan and make the Western Pacific a Chinese lake.

But a closer look tells us that China's future isn't all that bright. Its growth had already slowed dramatically before Covid-19 compelled the government to lock down major cities indefinitely. Farmland and energy resources are becoming scarce while the country is already grappling with water shortage. Thanks to its forced one-child policy of the Mao years, China is approaching a demographic catastrophe. It will lose 70 million working-age individuals over the next decade while gaining 120 million senior citizens. From the US to Taiwan, India to Japan, democracies are kicking Chinese firms out of their markets and creating multilateral coalitions to check Chinese expansionism. Also, China cannot ignore the surging anti-Chinese sentiment abroad.

If China's troubles make it less able to fulfil its dreams, the world must prepare for a more dangerous China. History tells us that such powers attempt to reshape the balance of power before the window of opportunity closes. Taiwan is the most likely target of this Chinese anxiety.

Till China was rising, it was content not to force the issue, and tried to entice Taiwan through peaceful means. But the Taiwanese do not want to be ruled by a genocidal dictatorship. After all, which freedom-loving people would want to?

Is Fascism Coming Back to Europe?

In the general election due to be held in a month's time, it is not unlikely that the Brothers of Italy party may win more votes than any other. Led by Georgia Meloni, the Brothers are rightwing and have the image of believing in a fascistic ideology. Benito Mussolini's Fascist Party came to power exactly a hundred years ago although that event was quite co-incidental. However, due to the records of Mussolini and Adolf Hitler, the thought of even a nationalist coming to power sends shivers down a European spine. Before their coming to power, nationalism was considered a desirable ideology because it represented love for one's country.

The metamorphosis of its image took place despite Hitler not using the expression 'fascist' for his party in any context. It was only Mussolini in Italy who called his party Fascist. The word was meant to convey 'unity' and not despotism. Incidentally, the really horrific crimes of WWII were committed in Germany and not Italy. Yet anything associated with nationalism or rightist thinking promptly reminds Europeans of fascism. The liberals in Europe call the regimes in Hungary and Poland 'illiberal', even if the latter are democracies. Communism and Leftist ideology suffered a demise some thirty years ago. And rightists are disapproved of, which leaves space for only centrists.

What was the fascist ideology? It certainly was not despotism.

The word "fascio" means a bundle or a bunch, implying unity. The movement was in response to the corruption, unemployment and the virtual economic collapse of Italy after World War I. The socio-economic conditions appeared to be ripe for a socialist revolution and fascism was a nationalist answer to pre-empt a communist takeover. Marxism was looked upon as depicting "class conflict". Capitalism still carried the stigma of "class exploitation" and was, therefore, a non-starter as a popular programme. To be effective, the answer had to be something that would prove attractive to the peasants, to the workers as well as to their unions. This was discovered in "class collaboration" as represented by fascism.

Prof Alfredo Rocco, the Minister of Justice in the Mussolini cabinet, set forth the gist of this new ideology in the course of a speech at Perugia in 1925. According to him, society does not exist for the individual; it is the individual who exists for society. Economic progress is a social interest and all classes of people should combine or collaborate to maximise production. The interests of the employers and the employed are identical. To ensure that this is practised, there must be a system of State discipline over class conflicts. Strikes and lockouts were alike illegal and punishable by heavy fines and in certain cases, by imprisonment.

Wherever possible, the employers and workers in each industry, trade or profession were organised together in syndical associations. Where it was not possible to form such syndicates, the unions and the employers' associations remained, but combined to form guilds to coordinate and ensure cordiality. If collective bargaining could not end satisfactorily, the disputes were referred to law courts assisted by experts. This is how class collaboration was conceptualised by the Fascist Party.

In practice, the economy was toned up by rearmament and public works. Soldiers were recruited in large numbers and so were workers in factories to produce arms. This would bring profit to the bourgeoisie who could then pay the proletariat well. Urban prosperity would increase demand for agricultural produce. What was left of the underemployed youth was absorbed by the armed forces. The promise to the entire nation was foreign conquests, which would bring booty. The Albanian adventure and the invasion of Abyssinia were two efforts to fulfil this promise until of course, World War II took place.

Another example of the practice of fascism or class collaboration, albeit on a much more limited scale, was in Spain under Gen Franco. Neither the Italian nor the Spanish experience is widely known in any great detail in India. What, however, the members of the intelligentsia are familiar with are the exploits of Adolf Hitler and his Nazi Party, whose full name was National Socialist German Workingmen's Party. It was founded by Hitler and his six comrades in Munich in 1920. The economic deprivation in Germany was much greater than witnessed in Italy.

No writing on fascism would be adequate without a mention of WWI, its end and the premature Russian surrender followed by the Bolshevik Revolution. Immediately following the takeover of Moscow by Lenin and his men, a civil war began between the Reds and the anti-Communists called the Russian Whites. It was a bitterly fought tussle which after a couple of years the White Russians lost, with most of them fleeing Russia.

Their defeat caused the Communists to be dreaded by the capitalists of Europe. As it happened, Mussolini and Hitler had founded their parties and had begun to resist the Communists on the streets of Berlin, Munich, Rome and Florence. But for them, the capitalist and industrial class might have been helpless. Similarly, without bourgeoisie money, Mussolini as well as Hitler might not have succeeded to the extent they did.

Israel and the World

A columnist in the national media has objected to what is termed Britain's 'grandstanding' on Gaza. This, according to this particular columnist, smacks of hypocrisy, because it was Britain that actually initiated the long saga of West Asian disputes and clashes, whose latest chapter is being played out on the Gaza strip.

The blame ought to be laid at the doorstep of Lord Arthur Balfour, who in the year 1917 was Britain's Foreign Secretary. Through the famous Balfour Declaration, he announced his country's support for a "national home for the Jewish people" in Palestine. It is not often realised that the British people were not anti-Semitic, certainly not as much as some of the nations of Continental Europe. One of their most distinguished Prime Ministers, Benjamin Disraeli, who served during the reign of Queen Victoria, was Jewish. A year after Balfour put forth his declaration, the Ottoman Empire, whose territory included the region known as Palestine, had lost the First World War, subsequent to which this West Asian region, centred on Jerusalem, passed into the hands of the Allied powers becoming a British protectorate. It became as much a part of the British Empire, as for example, India was at the time.

Pakistan was created as a result of a partition on 14 August 1947. The rest of the subcontinent became the dominion of India. The Hindus were aggrieved while the Muslims, wherever they were, celebrated the occasion with flowers and rosewater. Rather similarly, Palestine was partitioned on 14 May 1948, marking the end of British rule and the beginning of the modern state of Israel.

Palestine, or more specifically Canaan, was the home of the Jews—known in the ancient period as Israelites—even before Prophet Abraham blessed them, 2,000 years before Christ. Jesus and Christianity obviously came later, and Islam another 600 or more years later. Meanwhile, the Israelites later split into two kingdoms—namely Samaria in the North and Judea in the South. In due course, the Assyrian Empire conquered Samaria and later, the Babylonians came to establish sway over Judea.

Thereafter, Cyrus the Great, the Persian emperor, conquered and very kindly allowed the Jews to build their Second Temple in Jerusalem. Alexander of Greece and Macedonia captured Samaria and Judea in 332 BC, also ending Achaemenid Empire. In 64 BC, Imperial Rome conquered the Jewish land and made it one of the Roman provinces. At the time, Judea was predominantly a Jewish territory. Due to the harshness of Roman rule, the long exile of Jews from their land of origin, known as the Jewish Diaspora, began. In the bargain, the Christians soon outnumbered the Jews.

Thereafter, there began a long series of holy Crusades launched by the Christians to recover what they considered the land of Christ, or the "Promised Land". It was also the time when Islam came into prominence, with the Christian

Crusaders being ousted from Jerusalem.

In the early years of the nineteenth century, the Czarist rulers of Imperial Russia turned sharply anti-Semitic. Anti-Jewish pogroms became a weekly occurrence. This anti-Jewish sentiment spread across Europe, engulfing Germany under the Nazi regime in the twentieth century. Not having their own homeland left no choice for the Jews; they had no alternative but to somehow stay on in their host countries despite pogroms inflicted on them from time to time.

Jesus Christ was born a Jew and died a Jew. The only 'crime' he committed which led to his crucifixion by the Roman rulers of Jerusalem, was that one of his apostles, Judas, identified Jesus and revealed him to the Romans. Jesus, a Jew, was guilty in the eyes of the orthodox Jews for claiming that he was the son of God; in the Jewish realm, this is nothing but sacrilege, for no human being can claim to be divine and divinity cannot be conferred upon any human. On the other hand, the divinity of Christ and his being the son of God is central to Christian belief and religion.

The crucifixion of Jesus by the Romans at the behest of orthodox Jews sowed the seeds of discord and mutual hatred between Judaism and Christianity that persists to this day. The Christian Crusaders of Europe, whose armies marched into West Asia to free Jerusalem from the Muslims, also massacred thousands of Jews in the course of their two hundred year-long campaign. Anti Semitism, or more particularly anti-Jewish sentiment became entrenched across the Western world, with Jews being targeted because of their faith. They were forbidden to own land in Europe and the professions of money-lending, medicine and a few others remained the limited areas of economic activity they were allowed to be part of. The portrayal of the

Jew in Western literature and society became highly negative; for example, the Jewish moneylender Shylock in Shakespeare's epic drama *The Merchant of Venice*. The Holocaust of WWII, in which six million Jews were massacred by the Nazi regime of Germany, remains one of the blackest chapters of genocidal crimes against humanity.

The Israel-Hamas War in Perspective

The world is used to the spectacle of scholars, academics and social and political activists propagating and conferencing for global peace, but it is increasingly difficult to dismiss the notion that peace is little more than an uneasy halt between wars. While civilians somehow cling to some unreal hope, those in charge of the political destinies talk of peace, but actually build and sharpen their weaponry for the next bout.

In the land of origin of the three Abrahamic faiths, Judaism, Christianity and Islam, peace is currently the biggest casualty. Virtually everyone is concerned about the Israel-Hamas war. One, however, does almost immediately ponder as to how Tel Aviv was caught by utter surprise. Needless to add, the Israeli intelligence agency Mossad has been reputed to be one of the most efficient in the world, possibly the best spy agency. On balance, it appears that Hamas was conscious that there are groups within Israel that desire the Jewish homeland and country to further expand into a Greater Israel, as large and great as possible. Undoubtedly, the Hamas leaders themselves yearn to wipe the Jewish nation out of existence. With the help of friends and allies, it is likely that Hamas had been for a long time planning to strike a 'grand slam' at their Jewish neighbour.

The Israeli leaders too would like to get rid of Hamas from the country's neighbourhood. All of this lays the grounds for a conflict before the end of which the other side would supposedly be wiped out. A wounded enemy is more dangerous than one who hasn't been hurt. The question is whether Israel too sees the Hamas invasion and barbarity as a great opportunity for "setting things right" in the Middle East.

An organised Tel Aviv would certainly be functioning round the clock and will not give its adversaries any chance to destroy it. As luck would have it, Hamas perceived that its Jewish neighbour was divided over the issue of judicial powers enjoyed by the country's Supreme Court. They needed to be reduced or restrained so that the democratically elected Knesset or Parliament could assert its will more effectively. While the members of the Knesset could not readily reach a settlement, the people of the country took over and protested through public meetings and processions. Such scenes had not been seen ever before, and were being played out again and again on the streets of Tel Aviv and Jerusalem. When the adversary is divided, it is human nature for the other side to smell an opportunity.

The images of an Israel divided, in the streets of its cities, would certainly have held out the temptation, that this was the opportunity. A terrorist organisation like Hamas is unlikely to be foresighted. In fact, terrorism *per se* can seldom win for the simple reason that its adventures, however violent and apparently successful, do not capture territory. And without territory, there is no lasting victory. And yet, terrorist after terrorist gives up his life, merely to temporarily devastate places and people. Evidently, such men or women cannot be farsighted. Regardless, the attacks launched by Hamas on Saturday October 7 were thoughtless, to say the least. The consequences from Sunday onwards were foreseeable and yet, were not seen by the terrorist fighters of Hamas. It is not impossible that their escape route may, in an eventuality, be the Mediterranean Sea.

On the other hand, Hamas has gifted Israel with a justification to blame any country or organisation it chooses as a partner-in-crime that expresses even minimal sympathy for Hamas. Israel would also, and not without reason, feel justified to heap destruction on not only Hamas but also the palaces of Qatar (which reportedly fund the Hamas to some extent) and Iran's nuclear toys, as also bomb places in Syria, most of which are in ruins anyway because of the latter's civil war. Fortunately for Israel, ammunition began flying in from the USA; if necessary, advanced weapons would flow in. When Israel's Prime Minister says that his country will change the Middle East, he isn't bluffing.

Unfortunately, Israel—and India too—have been battling enemies who look upon war as a religious duty. Religiosity woven into war has the automatic effect of rendering the ensuing bloodshed all the more bitter. Such religious beliefs hold the promise of an eternal heaven with unending gratification of one's natural lust, in the pursuit of which the adherents of those dogmas have little hesitation in unleashing hell on earth.

For India, tightening our security, internal and external, in the wake of the war in Gaza will be imperative, for Hamas' initial boldness could well embolden elements in Pakistan to try something similar. This time, the Arab states have not supported Hamas, as several of them are seeking better relations with Israel and a different future.

The Russia-Ukraine Tango

Vladimir Putin visited Beijing in both 2024 and 2025 to further strengthen his relationship with China's strongman Xi Jinping. One sometimes wonders whether the Russian leader realises that he sits on vast spaces of land on the one hand; and stares at a declining population on the other. Does Putin remember that in 1969, his country fought a border war with China and had to lose a number of islands on the Ussuri river? One has to always bear in mind that in contrast to Russia, China has lesser land, but much more population. Siberia in Russia particularly has a lot of land, which will be naturally tempting to any land-hungry neighbour.

Notwithstanding this reality, Putin continues to wage a war that will soon complete nearly two and a half years. It is time to recover the republic which his late predecessor Mikhail Gorbachev allowed to secede in 1990. In a span of only thirty-two years, how can a mature nation like Russia have a change of heart like this? Incidentally, Ukraine had become a Soviet Republic only in 1922. Its government was reorganised by a constitution that was revised in 1937 by the Soviet Union, and amended in 1944, which gave Ukraine "the right to enter into relations with foreign states, to conclude agreements, and to exchange diplomatic and consular representatives with them", and to maintain its own military forces *(Encyclopaedia Brittanica).* Ukraine had its own membership of the United Nations; it was in fact, one of the founding members of the UNO along with seventy other international organisations. The Ukraine Ministry of Trade was permitted to establish agreements (exchanges) overseas; usually, these were limited to the socialist countries of Eastern Europe.

In the ninth century, the territory of Ukraine was known as the Kivian Roos, under the suzerainty of a duke of Varangian origin. This Kivian state extended westward and northward during the eleventh and twelfth centuries but was disrupted by a Tatar invasion during 1237-41. In due course, the succession of the ruler passed on to a Polish prince of the Piast Dynasty. When Poland and Lithuania became united in 1386, Ukraine came under their joint rule. In 1569, the Ukraine territory was separated from Lithuania and incorporated into Poland. The Poles were Roman Catholics and the religion of the Ukrainians was known as Eastern Catholicism.

Incidentally, from time to time, the Ukrainians were also known as Ruthenians. In the middle of the seventeenth century, Russia and Poland went to war against each other. As a result, in 1667, Ukraine was partitioned between Poland and Russia along the Dneiper river. The following year, i.e., 1668, the Ottoman emperor Sultan Mehmet IV managed to take over Ukraine and make it a protectorate. Ukraine thus fell under Ottoman suzerainity. In the course of the next couple of centuries, a united Ukraine assertetd its nationalism and the city of Kyiv regained some of its old glory.

During the course of World War I (1914-18) Count Georgy Bolorinsky was appointed the Governor-General of Ukraine, but because Russia sustained defeat in WWI, the short-lived glory came to an end. The Ukrainians saw their chance to achieve unity and independence and organise an independent government in Kyiv. They elected Srushevky as their president. Volodymir Vinnichenko became the Prime Minister and Symon Petlyura was the minister of war. The Russian communist regime of Vladimir Lenin tried to assert its rule by setting up a parallel government at Kharkov, but the Ukrainians insisted that they were a free and sovereign republic.

Meanwhile, the Central Powers led by Germany saw an opportunity for themselves and promptly occupied Ukraine. However, the Austrian governor could not last long in Lvov and had to hand over power on November 1, 1918. By January 23, 1919, Ukraine was again united and proclaimed itself an independent country with Kyiv as its capital.

The Russians, however, could not take their eyes off Ukraine. Not only the Red Army, but the White Russians too competed for power. On December 28, 1919, Lenin was so motivated as to address and pen a letter to the workers and peasants of Ukraine, in which he recognised the equality of the Russian and Ukrainian people, and suggested a treaty of alliance between the two. Such an alliance was concluded on 28 December 1920, in Moscow, signed by Lenin and Ra Kovsky; it was an act of incorporation. This incorporation was endorsed in his own signature by Marshal Josef Pilsudski, the then head of the Polish government.

It was on 20 December 1922 that the Soviet Union began to form a federation, which Russia, Byelorussia, Ukraine and the Trans-Caucasus came together in as the first step towards unification. Separatism, however, did not disappear in Ukraine and an underground Ukrainian military organisation called the UVO continued to simmer if not actively function. In fact, these Ukrainian nationalists looked to Germany for the realisation of an independent Ukraine. They hoped to provoke a Ukrainian revolution within the Soviet Union. On 30 June 1941, after Nazi Germany occupied Lvov, the Ukrainians proclaimed the restoration of their state as an independent republic.

After the death of Josef Stalin in 1953, Crimea was transferred to Ukraine; northern Bukovina and the Bessanabian districts of Hotin and Izmail were also incorporated into Ukraine.

Vladimir Putin is experienced enough to realise that statecraft works as much by diplomacy as by the power of one's arsenal. And diplomacy continually needs the blessings of friendship and goodwill. Is it possible that he doesn't know, sitting behind the walls of the Kremlin, that he has lost the goodwill of virtually the whole of Europe, and in fact the entire West? After attacking Ukraine, he has very few friends left. Ruling as he does, over 17 million kilometres of territory, why and how does he crave for bits and pieces of Ukraine? Especially so, when he should know that China can grab virtually what it likes of Siberia?

Europe Turns Rightward. But Why?

There is no doubt that Europe is leaning Right. National elections held in the Continent are bringing forth governments one by one, which can be called rightwing, but not fascist. The Netherlands has all but elected Geert Wilders, an unapologetic opponent of Islam. Giorgia Meloni, Italy's rightwing and nationalist Prime Minister, is going strong; she has thrown out China's BRI project and refuses to toe the European Union's line on immigration. Emmanuel Macron of France, who began as a centrist is turning right, much to the consternation of that country's socialists and leftists, while indications are that the far-right, anti-immigrant and anti-Islam Marine Le Pen might win France's next elections. President Emmanuel Macron has often spoken of the need of building a "Europe that protects". In a landmark 2017 Sorbonne speech, he had also called for "a sovereign, united and democratic Europe".

Finland has a strong rightwing Prime Minister, Petteri Orpo, who is no friend of unrestricted immigration. Hungary under Viktor Orban has already called the European Union a dysfunctional arrangement and no longer obeys its diktats. Now

Greece is throwing up rightwing politicians, who have opened their doors to Indian investments, but more importantly, Greece has stated that it will never be friends with India's enemies. Much to everyone's horror, the Alternative Fur Deutschland (AFD), a nationalist and rightwing German party is gaining ground in that country and might soon rule Deutschland. The AFD is reportedly a hard-right party opposed to the liberal and green environmentalist agendas of Germany's conventional political parties, and also their liberal stance on immigrants coming into Germany. The days of former German Chancellor Angela Merkel's 'welcoming' policies towards Turkish and Middle Eastern migrants are now more or less over.

Whether the new rulers admit it or not, they have been elected in response to a dread of Islam. The fascists had captured power between the two world wars, which itself had been a fearful response to the threat of communism.

In the context of World War II, Fascism/Nazism or class collaboration were conceptually appropriate to the growth of ideologies that propagated and promoted class conflict. Logically, the antidote to the fear of Islam should have been more and more influence of Christianity. Unfortunately, however, the grip of Christianity over the minds and hearts of Europeans, with the march of modernity and the progress of advanced learning and education, has dissipated. Education encourages thinking, and a thinking individual is not accepting any assertion without research or survey, preferably of an empirical nature.

Over and above this difficulty, three religions have competed with the same claim. To start with, Judaism, then Christianity and thereafter Islam have the same contention and beliefs thereof. To worship without being allowed to pursue spirituality or seeking an opportunity to see or feel the divine, is a very limiting and constraining experience. This can seem harsh to the thinking person.

Experts on Europe say that currently, only about 25 per cent of people in West Europe declare themselves as Christians, and only a small minority of even these people are church-goers. In other words, Christianity is in no position to help to keep Muslims out of the Continent.

Between the two world wars, waging class conflict was seen as something normal until it was countered with class collaboration. In its heyday, Christianity could have helped combat Islam. Today, the Europeans are abandoning their liberation and using nationalism to prevent further immigration from Asia and Africa. In a way, this is an about turn, because after WWII, nationalism had become unwelcome. Books were written to show that fascism was nothing but an intensification of nationalism and, therefore, was not welcome any longer. The coming together of Europe under the banner of the European Union (EU) was a demonstration of the post-WWII European opposition to nationalism.

The European far Right has been often accused by its Leftist and liberal critics of representing the worst things in European ideological traditions. These are namely, exclusive "nationalist essentialism", dogmatism that runs counter to the values that were bequeathed by the Enlightenment and political authoritarianism, which the Right is accused of re-energising. But the European Right today conveys a simple but powerful message, based on three core ideas: rediscovery of the nation and national identities; warning of the dangers of unrestrained immigration, particularly from Islamic countries, which is derided as xenophobia; and anti-politician, anti-establishment populism. In this regard, the far Right offers its followers an exclusive identity. The European Right has identified conventional politicians, i.e., the establishment as the culprits and advocates simple and now increasingly unavoidable solutions like throwing out unwanted foreigners, and an overthrow of the traditional political class. Right or wrong, good or bad, this seems to be catching on in today's Europe.

The Soviet Union was a superpower inhabiting a part of Europe's geography, to which also the European Union was an answer. An ideologically non-descript Russia, with its fifteen republics having seceded is no longer seen as an almighty threat. As a result, quite a few European experts may begin to consult crystal gazers to check up on the future of the European Union.

Economics

On the Eighth Anniversary of Demonetisation

Reportedly, there are some 50 petitions pending in the country's courts protesting the demonetisation of currency notes that was implemented on 8 November 2016. Understandably, this move by the Narendra Modi government continues to generate much talk. In all, I have witnessed three demonetisations and therefore, feel qualified to comment on the subject. In 1946, the old 1000-rupee note was demonetised. In 1978, high denomination notes were rendered invalid. We are today debating the 2016 decision.

In the pre-Modi era, it was widely believed that approximately 50 per cent of the Indian economy generated in the country could not be tapped at all for purposes of development. This black money had to be spent in less productive activities like land deals, property transactions and what not. Such money had to be spent quickly in order to keep it away from thieves and from income tax vigilance; its mention in any legal document was not possible. The tax-evaded money could neither be legally invested nor safely saved for even one's children, not to speak of national development. In brief, black was money only for the time being, in contrast to bankable money, which was actual wealth.

What was unusual about Indian black money was that it was reported to be manufactured in our neighbouring countries. West Bengal traders used to buy our toothbrushes readily; more especially if one did not write a bill and accepted cash. In the event the notes paid happened to be *jaali* (counterfeit) one would have been informed at which shop one could change them back to valid notes. When the thunderbolt of the 2016 demonetisation burst upon India, everyone up to the upper middle class was able to change their cash. Those who were hit were the people who had hoarded large sums of black money and could not change their notes. On the morrow of the occasion, many an economist or an intellectual began using the term "informal economy" for the black economy.

The result of the action was to get rid of the hoarded cash lying wastefully. However, its greatest service was to interrupt for a long time, if not forever, the printing of Indian currency notes in neighbouring countries. Simultaneously, smuggling of goods was significantly reduced. Nevertheless, demonetisation would have been a fleeting event, had it not been followed by the introduction of the Goods & Services Tax (GST).

I would like to bring in a personal experience in this particular regard. The sale of our toothbrushes increased within a fortnight. It was indeed a welcome surprise. Upon thinking further, we realised that quite a few of our competitors might not have maintained systematic records. Some of them were making brushes by simply sticking nylon into the plastic handles; they had brought these on a friendly basis from say, China. The history behind all this was that toothbrush manufacturing was for decades reserved for the small scale sector. In short, overnight, an informal activity turned into a formal sector one. Apart from sales tax, the additional fear was that from the GST website, the income tax department could also monitor how much of what product was being sold by whom.

An incidental but substantial advantage that emerged from the introduction of the GST was the drastic reduction in lorry transport time. Post-GST, an interstate lorry no longer has to stop at every state border. The lorry's photograph and registration are record by CCTV cameras. Earlier, the vehicle had to queue up at the state border to obtain clearance by the states' sales tax authorities. Up to 40 per cent travelling time has thus been saved.

Yet another advantage of GST has been the abolition of most other indirect taxes, starting from excise duty. Imagine the expenditure saved to the taxpayer on the one hand and the governments, beginning with the Centre, and ending with the states, small and big. Above all, the tax has taken India towards its goal of one country one tax. Moreover, demonetisation has helped India avoid its exploitation by its neighbours. The veteran political analyst and economist S Gurumurthy has likened the 2016 demonetisation to a "financial Pokharan", i.e., a nuclear strike against not only black money, but covert financial war against the nation.

Assuming that in the pre-Modi era, 50 per cent of India's economy was black; at least half this amount is currently being ploughed back into the economy as white money. In that sense, India's economy has become 25 per cent larger. It is also a necessary step towards making India a more modern economy, which is the first necessary step if we aspire to make the rupee into a convertible currency.

India as G-20 Leader

India was the leader of the G-20 group from December 2022 to December 2023. The presidentship of the G-20 catapulted India to the degree of prominence the country had not experienced before. However, G-20 leadership is only for one year. Thereafter, the dividend earned from the capital gained during this one year accrued.

The spontaneous conviction of most countries might well be that the peace will be, let us say, eternal. The "non-era of war" would endure indefinitely, to borrow somewhat from Prime Minister Modi's statement to Russian President Vladimir Putin. Thereafter, whether India becomes the world's number one power or not would be less important; the country would enjoy diplomatic dominance at least as long as peace lasts.

Every thinking person in the world today would be aware that the use of a thermonuclear weapon means widespread death and destruction. Yet, weaker or less responsible nations with nuclear weapons in their hands do not hesitate to threaten those countries of whom they are afraid, have ongoing issues or simply have scores to settle. It is possible that irresponsible leaders of such nations could well be tempted to use this weapon of mass destruction.

One hears much that is spoken and written in favour of diplomacy and statesmanship. However, it is essential that one recognises the historical fact that neither diplomacy nor strategy has prevented war. The Maginot Line of France failed to stop the German invasion in the summer of 1940, largely because German forces bypassed it through Belgium and the Ardennes. In Russia, invading armies—from Charles XII's Swedish forces in 1708, to Napoleon in 1812, and Hitler in 1941—were gravely weakened by not just the harsh winters, but also several other causes.

Something reminiscent of *dharma*, its inspiration as well as its deterrence could perhaps help to keep nations away from thinking of war and destruction. That the use of nuclear weapons is not merely destructive but also an evil, needs to be driven into the vast masses of people all over the world. How Hiroshima and Nagasaki were rendered burning hells in 1945 needs to be captured in record and displayed to all coming generations, especially in countries boasting of their nuclear arsenals. How murdering innocent human beings in such a manner is the worst *dushkarma* (misdeed) anyone, a group or nation can perpetrate, must be driven into the minds of people. How effective this conviction can be has been demonstrated through history in India.

The subcontinent was invaded via the Hindu Kush down the Khyber Pass and across the seas for no less than a millennium. There have been innumerable episodes of retaliation in justifiable defence by the Hindus. Yet, they suffered enormously in these invasions by an alien ideology and way of life; their temples were destroyed but they fought on. There are cultures that do not distinguish between killing the guilty and the innocent, but in butchering human beings and animals. Imagine desecrating a church or destroying cattle in an abattoir. The spread of *dharma* and awakening the perpetrators to the consequences of *dushkarma* would be the call that an international body can give to the comity of nations.

The world has also toyed with organisations and blocs, all for the stated purpose of achieving world peace and preventing war, but all such attempts have proved mirages, as the history of the world shows. The League of Nations following the end of WWI and the United Nations Organisation after WWII are examples that come to the mind. Then there are organisations like the European Union, BRICS (Brazil, Russia, India, China and South Africa) and various regional blocs around the world, whose stated purpose is to influence geopolitics and geoeconomics by proactively promoting the interests of the regions these blocs represent. Global peace is ostensibly sought to be achieved through trade and economics.

The G-20 being essentially an economic forum would have the primary duty to also awaken as many nations as possible to the crime of destruction. The country has already become the world's fifth largest economy and is one of the world's leading powers, though India does not seek to dominate others. Unless the hearts and minds of people are influenced, the darkest chapters of history would be written again and again.

Why Football Must Grow in India?

The riotous protest witnessed in Paris on the eve of the FIFA World Cup Football final in Qatar showed to what heights football can arouse emotions. It is the world's biggest sport with the maximum following and the enormity of the money it generates. In the year 2021, world football's earnings were estimated to be $600 billion, well over twice of what all other sports put together earn. Incidentally, in the USA, football is called soccer.

Football came to India earlier than cricket, which was initially promoted and patronised by princes, who sat on the thrones of states like Jamnagar, Baroda, Indore, Patiala *et al.* The legendary Ranjitsinghji became the Maharaja of Jamnagar. The national cricket team was generally captained by the maharajas, like those of Patiala, Porbander, Vizianagaram and so on. In short, cricket was a princely game, little connected with the soil of India.

On the other hand, football was the common man's favourite in eastern and southern India; the north was fond of hockey while the west tried to play cricket. The football hero of eastern India was Gostha Pal, who retired in 1936.

The central thrust of this submission is that some institution in our country should consider promoting football eventually on a national scale. The game is ideally suited for the common folk of India, whether in the cities, towns or villages. Football requires only about a sixth of the land area essential for cricket. Even in a small village, boys and girls can begin kicking the ball without much preparation; there is no need for mechanised equipment like steamrollers. There is no equipment other than the ball. Until some years ago, there was no need for the players to wear any shoes. The legendary Gostha Pal donned boots only during the monsoons. It is relevant to mention that football can be played at any time of the year. Europe considers it a winter game, whereas in India it is considered a summer-cum-monsoon sport. Apart from the player not needing much equipment, the team or the club too does not need to pour in large sums of money to prepare for the kick-off.

Football consumes less than two hours for a fulfilling game whereas cricket occupies more time. Gostha Behari Pal, (August 1896 - April 1976) was an Indian footballer who played as a defender. He was the first captain of the Indian national team and played during the 1920s and 1930s. Spending most of his career in Mohun Bagan, Pal is regarded the best player ever to have played for the century-old club. 'I see, you are Goshta Pal, the Chinese Wall'—Rabindranath Tagore, Asia's first Nobel Laureate, addressed Pal on meeting him after arrival of Mohun Bagan players in Shantiniketan. Nicknamed as "Chiner Pracheer" (The Great Wall of China), Pal was one of the best defenders of contemporary Indian football.

After his death, a statue was erected in memory of him at the Gostha Pal Sarani (named after him) in 1984, opposite to the Eden Gardens at Kolkata Maidan area. The statue was unveiled by then PWD minister Jatin Chakraborty. In 1998, a postage stamp dedicated to Pal was unveiled in Calcutta by India Post. Thus, he became the first Indian footballer to have a commemorative postage stamp in his honour. Later, within Mohun Bagan club tent, a museum was built in his name. Gostha Pal Championship, named after him, under the aegis of All India Football Federation's 'Golden Baby Leagues', was incorporated to include more children from Kolkata into the football culture.

Former FIFA president Sepp Blatter who visited India in 2007, had called the country a "sleeping giant" of world football, and wanted to awaken it. He called India "another market" for the beautiful game and endorsed the then upcoming franchise-based Indian Super League (ISL).

"Football has to keep on spreading throughout the world. We have seen success with the professional league in China, but I can inform you that we will have a professional soccer league in India," Blatter was quoted as saying in the magazine *Sports Business International* .

"This is another market for football, not a financial market but another market to grow our sport. There are 1.3 billion people in India, that's 1.3 billion people who want to play football now," added the head of the world football's governing body.

"Obviously, they like cricket and it's a good sport; let them play it, but it's not as good as football," Blatter went on to say.

Don't Succumb to Soft Emotions

In the course of his presidential address to the Muslim League on March 22, 1940, at Lahore, proposing the Partition, Jinah had said that the question of Hindu-Mohammedan unity was neither possible nor practicable. There was no finer Mohammedan in Hindustan than Hakim Ajmal Khan, but could any Muslim leader override the Quran? Also, what about the injunctions of the Hadiths? No Muslim could override them. He had quoted the *London Times* saying that "the differences between Hindus and Muslims are not only of religion but also of law and culture. They may be said to represent two entirely distinct and separate civilisations". He further said, "The only course open to them is to allow them to have separate homelands".

He had said it was extremely difficult to appreciate why the Hindus failed to understand the real nature of Islam and Hinduism. "They were not religions in the strict sense of the word, but were, in fact, different and distinct social orders. It was a dream that the Hindus and Muslims could ever evolve a common nationality. The Hindus and Muslims had different religious philosophies, social customs and literatures. Their views on life and of life are different. It is also quite clear that Hindus and Muslims derive their inspiration from different source of history. They have different epics, heroes in different episodes. Very often the hero of one is a foe of the other and, likewise, their victories and defeats overlap. To yoke together two such nations under a single state, one a numerical minority and the other a majority, must lead to growing discontent and the final destruction of any fabric that may be so built up for the government of such a state."

It is clear from many discussions in social media that some Pakistani citizens, in desperation born of the current crisis in that country, are suggesting that Pakistan should merge back with India. Many also say that Jinnah made a mistake in striving for and achieving Partition. There would be some in India, too, who would desire such a merger, for old times' sake. But such a re-merger is not desirable. One swallow does not make a summer, and in all, likelihood Allah the Merciful may lead Pakistan out of this crisis.

We in India remember the year 1991, when Prime Minister Chandra Shekhar, assisted by the then finance minister Yashwant Sinha, were dispatching gold to London every day against an IMF loan. It was only when P V Narasimha Rao became Prime Minister that New Delhi was able to retrieve the situation, including getting India's gold back.

We also remember how some 25 years ago the Pakistani per capita GDP had overtaken the Indian counterpart. Such ups and downs are the features of the history of many a country. No country merges with another at the advent of a doubt. In the case of Pakistan, such emotions may be understandable because it has undergone a demerger twice; once in 1947, from India, and again in 1971, from East Pakistan, which subsequently became Bangladesh. New Delhi should, therefore, not take the current emotional outbursts emerging from Pakistan seriously and should turn a deaf ear to such fleeting emotions.

The perennial problem of India is not the issue of the two religions Hinduism and Islam. The inescapable syndrome is the contrasting systems of logic, upon which the two faiths are based. Islam, as well as Christianity and Judaism, were founded and followed based on a system reminiscent of Deductive logic. This branch of logic begins with an assumed premise. In religion, this premise is the assertion that there is only one God and then the logic follows flawlessly. In sharp contrast, the backbone of Hinduism is Inductive logic, which begins with facts on the ground and moves upwards to a conclusion. This may not be a singular postulate, but merely an agreement to disagree. In the light of the difficulties, it would be useful to recount Dr B R Ambedkar who had written that 1920 onwards, India suffered a continual civil war (and in fact, continues to do so). Surely, India should not risk a repeat of that misfortune all over again.

Labour Reforms

Apropos of the article entitled "Managing Reform Risks" by A K Bhattacharya (*Business Standard*, 22 March 2023), given correct communication, there should be no risks. The loud and clear message to the trade union activists should be: the more the industries, the more the unions and greater your bargaining power. Political and trade union activists with a Marxist background understand this spontaneously. Karl Marx's initial idea was to expand the proletariat, so that "more and more workers of the world could unite". Thus, the communist hold over societies increases and the revolution comes nearer. This precisely is the essence of the Communist Manifesto.

As far as the worker is concerned, his instinctive motivation is that jobs should be so many in number that he obtains employment easily. His second objective is to obtain as high a wage as possible and incidentally, as little working time as possible. The third motivation is not universal, as all homes are not congenial, nor are all families; therefore, not all workers know what to do with themselves if they reach home early. One reason for a resort to drinking is leisure. Not every working person has access to a club, sports and games. The priority of trade union leaders is to have more and more numbers under their umbrella, although their public stance has to be worker welfare, workers' safety and comfort, more leisure, higher wages, etc. They do not particularly favour training of workers, mostly because contact between the employer or his managers and the workers is not advantageous to the union's control over its members.

One of the reasons for corporates often not being able to deal satisfactorily with their workers is insufficient contact, inadequate knowledge of worker ethos and trade union priorities. I am unable to think of any large company having on its board of directors a person with frontline experience of dealing with unions and their members. It is true that the late Naval Tata was an expert in industrial relations, respected also by the International Labour Organisation (ILO) at Geneva. But I doubt if he had an opportunity to deal with and overcome labour trouble at the factory level. Most corporate houses dealt with such worker problems through their labour officers.

1975 onwards, I had to revive the main factory in Kolkata of India's once second-biggest cigarette manufacturing company called National Tobacco. It was situated ten miles from the famous Writers' Building. Its troubles began in 1967, when the so-called *gherao* minister, Subodh Mukherjee, handled the Labour portfolio in West Bengal's United Front ministry. In the course of six hours on an afternoon in May that year, twelve officers were continually beaten. The minister stood outside so that the police could not go in to intervene. Calm could return only as late as 7.30 in the evening; ambulances were allowed inside to take the injured officers away to hospital. This was followed by a lockout that lasted for over a hundred days. The management was demoralised because its brands lost their markets; the company became weaker and weaker until its management landed in my lap eight years later.

I had no earlier experience of industrial relations. In my search of how to handle the situation, I found quite a few experts to advise on the basis of their theoretical knowledge of law, but no one who could suggest a strategy. At the time there were labour officers and experts, but they existed in separate domains. There was no one senior enough with field experience. Nevertheless, we were able to rationalise the workforce by some 35 per cent—860 men to be precise—which in the West Bengal of 1975 was unusual.

Times have changed. The concept of workforce trimming is widely called rationalisation or a "golden handshake". It also needs to be publicised how much indirect employment and wealth a modern factory or company creates. The popular focus even today is on the number of people directly employed. This might not exceed, in any cases, more than one worker for a crore of rupees of investment. To avoid misunderstanding as well as unjustified opposition, which is Bhattacharya's legitimate apprehension, a great deal of information needs to be widely disseminated, so that no clash or tension takes place out of ignorance of facts.

For example, in 1967, a clued-up management would not have declared a lockout. Apart from the loss of market to the company, a lockout helps the union and its members to stay united. In contrast, a strike leaves open the possibility of disunity setting in the workers' ranks. Many companies in Kolkata in those days had conceded a checkout system, whereby the management undertook to deduct from the workers' wages the union subscription and hand it over to the union. How absurd that the management should undertake financial responsibility and risk unpopularity with the workers for no return from the union?

The fear of the union at National Tobacco was such that the management had conceded 119 designations among a workforce of 2,360. The clear implication was that a worker with an 'X' designation would not touch the function of another worker, who would be designated 'Y'. The cigarette rolling department had four sections—each of them had one gum deliverer, who would fetch a drum of fresh gum. It took him no more than ten minutes to do so. But he would not help any other department, like fetching gum for any other section. When raw tobacco reached the factory by rail, a gang of fourteen workers would unload it. During the time, five other gangs would be sitting around. If two workers of the first gang were absent, no one from any of the free gangs would help. Two temporary workers from outside the factory would be called to help make up that day's shortfall in the workforce. This again, was a way of increasing employment.

Barter Trade and Currencies

Resentment against the dominance of the US dollar as a medium of payment for international transactions is no justification for another currency being pushed as an alternative. Commercially promoting one would have no objection. In any case, there are a number of alternatives already present except that none of them is as prominent as the dollar. The Swiss franc, the Japanese yen, the British pound are only three from the number available. Interestingly, India had innovated in the early years of Independence what it called the rupee or the barter trade with a number of countries. The most prominent participant was the Soviet Union followed by a number of its satellites plus Egypt, Iraq and so on.

This faster trade was inaugurated when Manubhai Shah was the Commerce Minister. Many years later he admitted that it was a mistake made in the process of finding a way out of hard currency shortage. Actually, it was not a mistake but an incomplete scheme and, therefore, it failed. Ideally, barter can happen and might be considered under appropriate circumstances, but it should have been among several nations and not between only two countries at a time, say India and Iraq without a third member. And it should have been operated with the help of a facilitating currency, innovated for this particular barter club of four or five members. Additional members, provided they had a similar interest could be admitted if they were found suitable. The central point here would be the congeniality of products or services amongst members of a particular club, so that normally, the congeniality of the items of trade can continue, or is in place at least for the duration of transactions. If this congeniality alters over a period, there should be a provision for setting up a closing account with the help of the facilitating currency agreed upon. The exchange rate of the facilitating currency vis-à-vis respective currencies of the members of the barter club has to be agreed upon at the outset, with mechanisms to handle market rate fluctuations too in place, especially with respect to a chosen hard currency. This ensures a system whereby not only can a member enter a club but also withdraw from it smoothly.

In the late 1970s, the Soviets could visualise that they were going to suffer from an acute shortage of hard currency. They, therefore, proposed that the value of their rouble be fixed. In its naiveté or perhaps under pressure, the Government of India agreed to Rs 18 as the permanent equivalent of a rouble. By 1990, the rouble's value had nosedived to such a nadir that the Russian currency then stood at no more than a few paise for one rouble. In the bargain, India lost crores of rupees in exports to the Soviet Union, and finally jettisoned the barter trade in 1991. During the heyday of the Indo-Soviet rupee-rouble barter, trade malpractices too would be rampant. For example, the handles of reading glasses manufactured elsewhere would merely be screwed on the main frame, and then be exported to countries like Russia for payment at the rupee-rouble rate, costing the country in millions of actual currency value. The Soviet Union also purchased the maximum quantity of tea in 1991, just before it went bust. Such fraudulent avenues have to be sealed off.

The one great essential for becoming a popular hard currency is the generation and sustenance of faith in that currency. It should be available in plenty and should not be prone to any abnormal inflation or deflation. The country's economy should be stable enough to absorb virtually any shock, and the currency should be free to be used by anyone in any country without restrictions. For example, Zimbabwe is reported to have replaced its earlier currency, which became a victim of hyperinflation, with the US dollar. Incidentally, most of us have forgotten that the Indian rupee was the currency of a number of West Asian principalities until after World War II. Evidently, the faith these principalities had in the British Crown did not get transferred after Independence.

The remarkable feature of the dollar has been its stability. Since the global financial crisis of 2008, the quantum of dollars in circulation in the world is six to seven times that of the amount available before the crisis. Yet, the dollar has not suffered undue inflation on this account. The explanation for this phenomenon lies in its universal demand, as opposed to only a national requirement. The Federal Reserve, which manages movement regarding the dollar, is a completely autonomous body and is never interfered with by the US government in Washington DC.

All in all, a currency cannot be converted or shaped into a hard one merely by wishful thinking. Not only should the economy of the country be stable, association with such an economy and country should lend consistency and stability to the user country. A beginning can best be made by aspirants setting up clubs or conglomerates of congenial trading. If over the course of time such groups can demonstrate success, faith would begin to build up. If India is successful in this, it would have laid down long-term macro-economic stability as well.

GDP or Net Tax Collection as a Measure of a Country's Economy

A retired professor of economics recently told me that Bangladesh has overtaken India. Its per capita GDP (gross domestic product) has overtaken that of India. Bangladesh's GDP was $2,620 and India's was $2,610 a couple of years ago. That made the average Bangladeshi, slightly richer or at least better-off than an average Indian. Fair enough, but then why did Prime Minister Sheikh Hasina come to New Delhi to borrow 9.5 billion dollars from the Indian government? The professor replied: 'to further develop the Bangladeshi economy!'

Over the last ten years or so, discussing the GDP of countries has become fashionable for comparing one country's economy to another's. And the prosperity of the people has begun to be the major yardstick by which to measure the GDP per capita. Hard-headed businessmen, who have handled larger issues, would rather begin by asking for a country's total annual tax collection whether by the Centre or the States or even by the municipalities. They would then proceed to inquire about the total governmental, all three levels including the municipalities, and deduct this total from the total taxation, including charitable or social welfare expenses. If there is a surplus at the end of the arithmetic, that would be the country's surplus or the net annual income. This figure can be divided by the number of citizens to arrive at the per capita surplus. Then check the government's total data, local as well as international. The total data may be divided by the number of citizens to arrive at the data per capita. This method of calculation should give a clearer picture of the country's financial situation.

A country's total taxation less its expenditure is not always its surplus and perhaps could be a deficit. Years ago, the then Pakistani High Commissioner and his wife had dinner with us. In the course of our conversation, the lady happened to say that in Pakistan, very few people pay any tax, to which the husband added that we would be alright so long as they kept getting foreign aid and could afford to import all kind of items including beef. The High Commissioner continued, that in the early years of the 1960s, President Ayub Khan, asked his people to abstain from eating meat one day a week. This was to reduce the consumption of meat and fish. That means there was already a shortage of meat.

Years later, I come across a book, *The Long Divergence: How Islamic Law Held Back the Middle East* by Professor Timur Kuran. The gist of his contention was that the Islamic personal laws and their effect on the Muslim mind was to distract them from financial wisdom. Professor Kuran sounded anxious for the continued health of the Pakistani economy.

Incidentally, in 1980, Pakistan was ahead of India in dollar terms; maybe thanks to foreign aid. However, would all the factors be reflected by quoting GDP numbers even then? Net taxation should be a much better reflection of the economic condition of the country.

At this point it would be interesting to recall the views of Prime Minister William Pitt the Younger who was elected continuously as Britain's Prime Minister for twenty-two years at the turn of the eighteenth century. His plan was to build up a huge governmental surplus; so large that in the course of years, the British government could run Great Britain with the help of the interest earned by the surplus without levying taxes from the people. Before his plan could succeed, it was unfortunately interrupted by the emergence of Napoleon Bonaparte. William Pitt's plan of ensuring a sound economy was upset by deficit financing.

Controlled deficit financing is useful for developing an economy but it is injurious to print money merely to fill the gap between excessive expenditure and insufficient taxation. A friend of mine who visited Brazil some years ago discovered that its five-star hotels did not have any fixed tariffs; he was informed every morning as to the day's new rate according to inflation in the country. This was due to increasing expenditure and insufficient taxation. When I visited Myanmar some years ago, from the hotel down to children selling trinkets, most preferred American dollars to the local currency. Incidentally, Zimbabwe has replaced its traditional currency due to hyperinflation and replaced it with the American dollar. Now it has no currency of its own!

Need for National Management Studies

According to those who know, there are approximately 4,000 institutions devoted to teaching management across the country. Some specialise in finance, others in human resources, development, and business management of modern communication, etc. Marketing is such a wide discipline that there are dedicated management institutes for this. Others are more spread out in their curricula. Some are government-promoted, while others are promoted or sponsored by private companies, especially large corporate houses. Yet, not a single institution teaches management of the country. National management should have been considered the most important, as it would affect every citizen.

There are so many countries across the globe; their population, i.e., the total number of people in the world is a little above 8 billion. It is true that the science of management began to be developed only about a century ago. The idea of developing management studies came into its own when some German army officers of World War I thought of analysing the efficiency of their army. One such study threw up an interesting and important fact. This was that there were four non-combatants who were operational for one frontline soldier to be able to fight efficiently. In contrast to this, the British frontline fighting soldier had ten non-combatant personnel supporting him.

These two ratios showed that organisationally, the Deutsches Heer, or the Imperial German Army was two-and-a-half times more efficient than its counterpart across the North Sea.

The militaries of other countries too carried out similar studies, out of which the phrase "tooth-to-tail ratio" was born; the teeth being the fighting soldier. From this ratio grew some commercial houses which divided their employees into staff that earned revenue and others who carried out general tasks.

Business management schools began taking off especially after World War II. But they did not proliferate until the 1970s into hospitals and hotels, colleges and schools. The best teacher became a headmaster; the most distinguished professor became the principal and the best doctor became the superintendent. Jaslok Hospital in Mumbai, I believe, was the medical institution planned with the principles of management prevailing then.

For quite a long time, administration was mixed up with execution and/or management. There was no conscious realisation that the first function of the former is discipline, whereas that of the latter is achieving results. This lack of awareness of the differences has brought down the economies of many countries. More countries are mismanaged than managed properly. India, was unaware, until 2014 that it had to be managed—call it governed—and not merely administered. Although, we must give credit to India's first Prime Minister Jawaharlal Nehru that he was conscious of planning from the outset, i.e., the beginning of his tenure as Prime Minister. He did not wait for the newly independent country to elect its first Parliament; he established the Planning Commission by a cabinet fiat. That a plan had to be implemented and not merely published on paper was the purpose of this body. In the bargain, Yojana Bhavan functioned somewhat like the Gosplan of the (former) Soviet Union.

Nevertheless, India was governed better than the countries in our immediate neighbourhood, most of which are on the verge of becoming bankrupt. The example of China is unique. The scale of its growth and development on the morrow of Mao Zedong's passing has been undoubtedly phenomenal. The inspiration provided by his successor Deng Xiaoping was outstanding by any measure, but somewhere down the years, the efforts and exertions of the regime in Beijing violated a fundamental principle of management. That is: no country or economy should produce anything indefinitely unless there is a market. However, some economic wizard must have suggested that for some years to come, the economy could grow by pegging its fortunes on the real estate industry. The Chinese regime began with roads and parks, stations and airports, and ended with residential apartments. This mega building programme did increase the need for cement, steel, bricks and other goods, plus employ a large number of people as workers. With real estate, building became an engine of rapid growth and the programme was pursued with gusto. Exports were built up on the back of this activity thereafter, with the growth of apparent financial surpluses.

Some national assets were exchanged in return for hard currency, but the Chinese regime ignored this. Many a multinational as well as non-resident jumped on to this bandwagon. Money was borrowed through banks, the source being deficit financing. The sale of millions of new residential apartments rested on hope rather than demand. Unsold apartments cannot go on propelling the economy beyond a point.

Not many in the ruling elite of Pakistan showed interest in understanding economics. The rulers did not take conscious note of the fact that neither wing of their country, east or west, had much industry. The private sector had established a few jute mills at Narayanganj near Dacca (now Dhaka). There were some cotton mills in West Pakistan, but few entrepreneurs. During the regime of Ayub Khan, Pakistan boasted of some twenty-two elite and rich families who could supposedly propel the country's economy. But it was not realised that fourteen out of these families were Gujaratis; either Memons or Khojas, who had migrated there after Partition. There was very little local talent. Pakistan's politicians were busy with their intrigues and took little interest in their country's industrialisation. The one person who understood this situation was Pakistan's first president Iskander Mirza, a descendant of Nawab Siraj-ul-Daula of the Battle of Plassey. Mirza was also the first Indian to become the King's Commissioned Officer. In his opinion, the government should avoid being influenced by either religion or the military. Religion led to bias, while the military was in its element during a war, but had no understanding of a civilian economy. Unfortunately, Pakistan made both these mistakes.

The country was quick to respond to the American call to join the Baghdad Pact, which later came to be known as the Central Treaty Organisation (CENTO).

Foreign aid into Pakistan began flowing and imports became liberal, which made any initiative in indigenous manufacturing unnecessary. Field Marshal Ayub Khan took over as president in 1958, for ten years. A little later, General Zia-ul-Haq ruled for another decade after grabbing power in 1977. Yet another general, Musharraf, ousted an elected government in 1999 and ruled Pakistan for the next eight years. Thereafter, it is the army that has ruled Pakistan directly or indirectly. By 2016, aid from the USA virtually dried up and the generals did not know where to look for aid, except China. Beijing, however, demanded interest plus guarantees, which included forfeiture of territory in the event of non-replacement. All in all, Pakistan violated every rule of management.

The Sri Lanka story is very different, but again, its government did violate fundamental rules for the country to suffer. Myanmar has been under military rule since 1958. Bangladesh has an inherently weak economy, while Nepal is yet to experience full development.

The examples that shine when it comes to national management are Germany and Japan after World War II. The city state of Singapore stands out as the brightest jewel, although a small one, its master jeweller being the legendary Lee Kwan Yew. India has today the best government it has had since its independence. Before we conclude, we should draw readers' attention to the USA, which is a systemic rather than a managerial success. Its constitution has given the country a governmental structure that is unique. Its separation of powers, legislative, executive and judicial, is such that, within reasonable limits, no matter the quality of the individual governor(s), the country has kept flourishing for over two-and-a-half centuries. This merits a separate study.

Work 70 Hours a Week

Narayana Murthy has rightly highlighted the need for every Indian to work hard, harder than he/she has been doing hitherto. Without that extra effort, our economy cannot catch up. Our country, certainly many areas, has fewer assets and more people, adding up to poverty. To exit this rut, we must use assets more productively and cost-effectively. One answer lies in, wherever possible, more shifts or work hours out of the twenty-four given by nature. Due to old habits, we are influenced by sunrise, sunset, daylight and darkness. In Scandinavia, this was justified to an extent prior to the discovery of electricity. In those times, there were days especially in Norway when the sun did not set. The country was called the Land of the Midnight Sun. Similarly, in winter, there were days when the sun hardly rose. As a result, the spring, summer and autumn were associated with hard work and winters were for hibernation. Little wonder that European civilisation flourished in Greece, Italy and Spain while the North did not progress commensurately. The scenario changed drastically with the advent of electricity, enabling functioning at night about as efficiently as in daytime.

Conditions in India are different. Our problem is more people and lesser assets. For the large population we have, we haven't yet been able to build up adequate assets. One of the easier paths to progress is for us to utilise whatever assets we have intensively and thus also give more opportunities to our people by providing more employment. In many parts of the country, there are complaints about the problem of either unemployment or underemployment.

To take a concrete example, let us look at the judiciary. We have no shortage of lawyers; in fact, many younger ones complain of being without briefs. Moreover, there is an enormous backlog of pending cases. On the other hand, courts cannot function for as long as other offices because judges have to read the petitions and affidavits before hearing the cases. Similarly, the advocates have a great deal of backup work; their job does not begin and end with simply pleading in court.

Six hours, including lunch-break, five days a week is all the duration a court sits. Then there are summer vacations plus other breaks during the year. Why cannot, therefore, these courts have two shifts? The first shift ends at 16.30 hrs; the second can begin at 17.00 hrs and go on till 23.00 hrs. There will be any number of advocates to whom the second shift may not suit. Be that as it may, there would be many others who would prefer the evening shift; some might also agree to alternatively work in both shifts.

Judges may be given a choice; to begin with, they may be paid an extra allowance for late shifts. An incidental benefit would be that the courts would insist that the government improve the law and order situation, so that the working lawyers and judges are not waylaid or otherwise harmed. The greatest benefit, of course, would be to the litigants, who wait endlessly for their cases to be heard and concluded.

Justice delayed is often said to be justice denied, but seldom is it acknowledged that delayed justice imposes exorbitant costs on the nation, especially when developmental projects are delayed by litigation and become expensive due to the resultant inflation. It has not been written in any scripture that daylight is for work and night exclusively for sleep. In fact, in a largely warm country like ours, it may be more comfortable to work at night than day.

Narayana Murthy's formula of seventy work hours a week, if implemented, might actually reduce employment opportunities. More hours per week would mean fewer working persons. In a warm climate, working ten hours a day may be strenuous for some people. Moreover, with the increasing incidence of automation, the number of persons required per task would be lesser. Already, the number of jobs *per se* is under 50 per cent of the employable population in the world. The rest are self-employed. This ratio is likely to intensify against more and more jobs, which is likely to further reduce due to automation.

People are mostly prisoners of habit. All these years most domestic air flights usually began taking off at six in the morning and would halt operations at ten in the night, whereas, international flights could and did fly round the clock. No one could explain why this underutilisation of domestic aircraft was allowed to persist. Lately, we find that some domestic flights begin at 5 am and continue till 11 pm.

Whether some of us agree or disagree with Narayana Murthy, he certainly has done the nation a service in conveying the message that investments and industrialisation are not the only avenues of rapid economic progress. The people as a whole must also get down to hard work. The other factor that needs attention is that there cannot be a jumbo formula for India. We must recognise that the people of each state or region have different aptitudes and so does their agro-climate.

Lost to Economics

National dailies have reported that the Hindu community in Sind (Pakistan) are going to organise rallies which would converge on the Sind Assembly building. The objective is to protest against the rising incidence of forced religious conversions, abductions and child marriages of Hindus. The umbrella organisation under whose auspices this protest rally is to be held is the Darawer Ittehad, whose leader is Faqir Shiva Kuchi. That such protests and rallies have to be held clearly show that the Pakistanis have not yet learnt their lesson even after the acute economic crisis they are undergoing. Years ago, they should have discovered that unless they changed their ways, they would be headed towards such a crisis.

If only Pakistan had paid heed to sound common sense, of which there is never any dearth in the form of theses, literature and articles, they would perhaps have managed to escape the grip of the crisis they are facing today. Of all people, Jinnah would have known this the best; in his defence, one could say that he was sick when independence came in 1947, and died in a year's time. Not an inconsiderable proportion of Halai

Lohanas in Saurashtra converted to Islam. Similarly, Kutchi Lohanas converted to the Sunni sect of Islam; today, they are known as Memons. A significant number of Brahmins of north Gujarat, centered around Siddhur, became converts to Islam and are known as Bohras. They too developed a business aptitude. Many among these three communities migrated to Pakistan. Most of the business families in Pakistan were from this community. Arguably, this is one clue that a mainstream Muslim is not a natural businessman.

In the subcontinent, Muslim wealth was more in land and much less in business for the same reason. But not many Muslims notice this lacuna, except the likes of Prof Timur Kuran, an American scholar of Turkish origin. But before we come to him and his explanations, one factor of *taqlid* (orthodoxy) and its associate effects needs to be factored in. Education was not sufficiently encouraged in the community and certainly not among its womenfolk. An uneducated mother is often unlikely to realise the value of education. And a less educated society is unlikely to appreciate the value of economic education. This, in turn, causes a relative lack of awareness of the importance of business and industry.

Prof Timur Kuran, in his book *The Long Divergence: How Islamic Law Held Back the Middle East*, tells us that in the year 1000, the economy of the Middle East was at least as advanced as that of Europe. But by 1800, the region had fallen dramatically behind in living standards, technology, and economic institutions. In short, the Middle East had failed to modernise economically as the West surged ahead. Prof Kuran cites the factors of frozen *waqf* assets which carry prohibitions of any change in their inheritance, a dominant medieval legal system. Transformations were happening elsewhere but the mechanisms that fuelled the ascent of the West, kept the Middle East in a state of political and economic backwardness, and still continues to do so, the region's oil wealth notwithstanding. Its flourishing would have been made possible only with Western technological and managerial assistance. Prof Kuran's analysis concludes that several self-enforcing elements of Islamic law-contracting provisions, inheritance system, marriage regulations—jointly contributed to the stagnation of the Middle East's commercial infrastructure.

Pakistani physicist Pervez Hoodbhoy in his article in *Physics Today*, published in 2007, laid out the stark reality of education, particularly science education in the world of his faith. Islamic countries have nine scientists, engineers, and technicians per thousand people, compared with a world average of forty-one. Of the (roughly) 1.6 billion Muslims in the world, only two scientists have won Nobel Prizes in science (one for physics in 1979, the other for chemistry in 1999). Let us also take Pakistan's case, which is in dire economic straits today. From 1951 to the 2020s, the country received over $80 billion from the United States alone, aid from other countries/agencies in the West and its Middle Eastern patrons being excluded. One would naturally ask: where did all that aid disappear, given the perilous condition in Pakistan today.

One of the most far-reaching consequences of Pakistan's wars with India in its futile quest to wrest Kashmir has been the wide-scale economic slowdown in that country. The 1965 war ended whatever economic growth Pakistan had experienced during the early 1960s. Its defence spending has risen to nearly 80 per cent of its GDP, leaving nothing for development.

Cultural

Sermon on the Mount

Prime Minister's Independence Day speech a couple of years ago reminded one of the 'Sermon on the Mount' presumably delivered to Prophet Moses and his Judaic followers on their deliverance to Israel. The contents were not necessarily similar but their import were comparably classical. In twenty-five years time the PM wants India to be a developed country. Until the last century, we would constantly hear that India was a developing economy, belonging to the Third World. Today, the open objective is to be a part of the First World by the year 2047.

This a sharp and clear objective for the citizens to pursue, especially its leaders. Presently, many of them are obsessed with distributing freebees in order to win elections. This is a waste of wealth which should be deployed for economic growth. To elucidate this point, take demonetisation followed by the introduction of Goods & Services Tax. The first was a loud and clear message to people to keep away from hoarding tax evaded wealth because it cannot be productively deployed for developmental activities. The GST was a very constructive, on-going follow-up on retaining surplus wealth and deploying it for growth. Many citizens, habituated to hoarding their surpluses, still cannot see these two measures in this light.

This obstinate mentality which afflicts not only the wayward but also some academics and intellectuals would be one of the enduring roadblocks to the Prime Minister's march towards First World status. Apart from distancing our people from mental roadblocks, it is necessary for everyone, especially the rulers, to undergo an intellectual revolution, whereby unethical and stubborn old ideas are rejected spontaneously and not merely by fear of the Enforcement Directorate, Income Tax Inspectors, Central Bureau of Investigation and other agencies. The other psychological change required is to acquire confidence and overcome an inferiority complex. To give an example, I have a friend resident in Chittaranjan Park who was delighted that I may visit Dhaka to attend a wedding. His advice to me was to go, and see how a poorer neighbour had overtaken the Indian economy comprehensively. A couple of decades ago, there were Indians who believed that Pakistan had overtaken us in terms of economic points. The PM asked the people to shed any vestige of a slavery complex that might have been acquired inadvertently over the last many centuries. Indians of older generations did betray a readiness to concede the superiority of a foreigner, say a white person. At the same time, they were equally ready to come in the way of their friends and colleagues getting ahead by competition.

Being aware of one's own legacy is often the best way to feel self-confident. Other than political performance in the centuries past, Indians have a great deal to be proud of. In fact, had we not been a great civilisation we could not have survived the blows of so many foreign invasions. A great deal of our legacy is on display in buildings, temples, literature, epics and so on. Treat our united diversity as a source of strength and see how the variety adds power to team India—such a team would be a winning team especially if we keep our motherland as our first love and our priority. And of course we must resolve to be always free and not go under a conqueror.

There is nothing that Indians cannot achieve if they collectively make up their mind. Until 2014, for example, we had not paid much attention to cleanliness. But once we decided on *Swatchh Bharat* we have come a long way; the same with electrification of our villages and a number of other things. How quickly we have succeeded. So with manufacturing our toys and importing as few of them as possible. We resolved and we achieved.

Look at our frontiers today and contrast them with how weakly defended they were in the past. The secret of the success was our will power and sincere application. Now if we encourage our womenfolk to come more and more forward, India would progress much faster. They comprise a huge reservoir of India's strength which is lying untapped and, in effect, wasted. Turning to digital technology, luckily we caught the bus in time. See how soon we will derive great advantage in this competing world. All in all, India is strong and resourceful and will do well. Remember our single-minded aim to become a developed country by 2047!

We have not had the benefit of a visionary leader before. I believe one of the great secrets of American success has been the lack of dynastic inheritance even in their enormous corporate world. Hence it has been called again and again a land of opportunity.

Swami Ramdev and Allopathy

If all the medical experts knew the background of medicine in India, the current controversy might not have taken place. For centuries, India subsisted on Ayurveda and Unani (or Greek) medicine. The latter came to India via the Islamic invasions. They are still operating, unfortunately, without research and development. Lately, an effort has been launched near Sarita Vihar in Delhi with government support.

The other schools in our country are Homeopathy, Naturopathy and Allopathy, the latter alone is a beneficiary of research especially on a grand scale in a number of western countries. Ayurveda suffered a decline in the late nineteenth century in the absence of research and development. For example, Sushruta was as great a name as Charaka and was often referred to as the father of Indian surgery. Charaka had confined himself to pure medicine, mainly to gastronomy. It is said that he dedicated himself to gastronomy and the treatment of the alimentary canal without ever opening an abdomen. Ayurveda was able to be the backbone of healthcare through ancient and medieval times, until the nineteenth century, because it was a discipline for ensuring longevity rather than merely treating the symptoms of illness. Scholars have claimed it was a science of life; not merely to cure the sick but also to make the healthy, healthier. *Chyawanprash* is a simple example while *Rasayana* or rejuvenation its advanced face.

Until Allopathy took long strides in the early decades of the twentieth century, Ayurveda commanded its place. It had, for instance, *Serpina* for treating high blood pressure while Allopathy had no answer except placing live leeches on the patients' forehead to draw out blood and reduce its supply. My grandfather died at the age of 45 because of nephritis which made his kidneys dysfunctional. His final treatment was four weeks each in Vienna and London; this was in 1933. There was no antiseptic nor any antibiotics.

The discovery of antiseptics was a blow to Ayurveda; while that of penicillin during World War II proved to be a body blow. Yet, Indian scholars have not strategised the recovery of this science of life. Our science of life—Ayurveda—is potentially a champion of Indian civilisational revival and deserves our serious attention. Its concept of positive health care must be fully discovered. Who does not wish to live well and long? When I began to work I was twenty and it was considered to be too early. My employers retired its staff and executives at 55. Today, those retired at sixty complain about how to occupy themselves. Most of them are fit to continue working. A death in the early seventies is considered tragically young. Around Independence, sixty was an acceptable age to wind up one's life. Life span expectation has jumped by twenty years in well-to-do families.

The new challenge before Ayurveda, or any other school of treatment, is how to make the lengthening of lives more interesting and more enjoyable. Ayurveda and Rasayana aim for rejuvenation. It was a two-month treatment in a well-shaded camp. The two central thrusts were to keep clearing the bowels and scrupulously avoiding sunlight. Naturopathy can work wonders. I have witnessed my cousin being made to lose weight and how! When her therapy began she was eighteen years old, weighing 216 lbs. In the course of twelve months the weight came down to 130 lbs. The medicines were few, the diet was strict for six days in the week. Once a week she could have even a bar of chocolate.

In a country with poor people, Homeopathy can work wonders. In some persons, a few drops of its medicines work wonders all for a few rupees—no pain, no injections, no surgeries. The Germans invented it and they must be generously complimented. Unfortunately, hardly anyone has pursued it with research. Hence, this wonderful cure has not gone very far. Nevertheless, the system deserves encouragement and greater patronage.

Incidentally, Homeopathy is so named because it is not an antagonistic treatment. It is sympathetic in the sense that the medicine aggravates symptoms of the ailment in the hope that they get pushed out of the body. Most other schools of medical treatment are known to be antagonistic which means attacking the symptoms in the hope of killing them. Ayurveda and Naturopathy are different in the sense that one takes a broad view of the patient's whole life, while Naturopathy again leans on nature and tries to bring the people in step with what nature expects.

Ayurveda is given the credit for innovating the vocation

of nursing. Both male and female nursing began centuries ago although the practice took a long time to spread. In short, Ayurveda has a record of being innovative and of sustaining the whole Indian civilisation. It takes an overall original approach to the science of life.

Humanity Needs to Go Vegetarian

Humans began eating animal meat when man had not learnt how to grow grain, vegetable or fruits. He knew no agriculture at all. Yet, in many places animals might have lived nearby and therefore, were easy to catch and kill. To make his food tastier, and easily accessible, he took to meat-eating. I say man, because it is my impression that women crave less for meat than men. This is so in India and impressions gathered in Europe. This could be due to traditions that began with man going out to hunt while the woman stayed at home.

There is no doubt that nature meant humans to be vegetarians; or else, their teeth would not be flat, unlike those of the carnivores, which have long, canine teeth, which are very helpful in tearing into the flesh of animals. The elephant, rhinoceros, cow, horse and buffalo all have flat teeth and have remained vegetarian. Evidently, it was not a question of nutrition, protein or muscle. The vegetarian animals named here live off grass or leaves. Yet, they are all strong, muscular and healthy. The explanation probably would be that the digestive system of natural vegetarians would find protein or some similar nutrient that provides the elephant and the rhino with the strength and muscle that it has. This phenomenon is demonstrated in the human world as well, where there are champion wrestlers, who are vegetarian, as well as other sportsmen and sportswomen. Yet, it is a popular belief that meat-eaters are naturally stronger and more muscular than their vegetarian counterparts. The argument is that the protein from meat is more readily absorbed in the human body than from lentils or *dal*.

In my view, the cruellest side of meat-eating can be imagined if one were to imagine or realise that someone has killed his/her child merely to eat its meat. This argument of mine has been countered once or twice by posing a counter-argument that the modern way of delivering meat is to produce it from a piggery; pigs are bred, fattened and then slaughtered for delivery to the market. My reaction has been that a life is a life, no matter how it is born and bred. From the point of view of food, it must be remembered that the animal, before being slaughtered, consumes 900 kilos of vegetation and grains before delivering a hundred kilograms of meat. These figures are merely to illustrate that the ratio of meat and grain is 9:1. Fearing a possible food shortage, the Indian government has prohibited any export of wheat.

The caution stems from climate change, that has caused unpredictable changes in the sequence of seasons. In some areas of the globe there have been flash floods, while there have been widespread droughts in other regions. Both the phenomena, floods and drought will be a hindrance for normal food production. This makes avoiding meat-eating vital. One either saves nine kilos of wheat by avoiding meat or consumes a disproportionately large quantity of food grain for obtaining only a kilo of meat. Most estimates tell us that a vegetarian diet means 2.5 times less carbon emissions than a meat diet. Other examples, too, serve as illustrations of this fact. By eating vegetarian food for a year, we can save roughly the same amount of emissions as a family keeping a small car off the road for six months can.

The world's population is set to rise above 9 billion by the year 2050. A meat-eating life undeniably means that we are gobbling up the earth's resources faster than we can replenish them. At our current rate of consumption, which certainly includes non-vegetarian food, we shall need three planets to be able to sustain our current levels of living. Where will we find them?

For a Hindu, his/her universe includes all living beings. To kill an animal is murder, big or small. To do so merely to enjoy a sumptuous meal is considered heinous. The resulting *bhagya* (fate) of such a *karma* would be drastic. The average individual does not think things out. The crime, therefore, is beyond the average person's imagination.

In the Hindu ethos, the soul is an entity that keeps transmigrating from one living being to another through an endless cycle of birth, death and rebirth. This is the reason a Hindu is not easily driven to kill another being, even birds and animals. In fact, Hinduism is arguably the only way of life that worships animals and plants. Western countries have lesser regard for animal life. Even the Western world is realising that there is *karmic* inter-connectedness in this world. Globally too, the realisation is growing that genuine peace and a cessation of human conflict is not possible without compassion for all living beings. Turning to a vegetarian way of life is the simplest and yet most effective way of achieving this goal.

On Rishi Sunak

When Rishi Sunak, was chosen as the Prime Minister of Britain, he was not the choice of all British people, but was a child of desperation. Most leaders in his shoes would instinctively prioritised protecting what his predecessor Boris Johnson described as "the best job in the world". More so, because he had been selected, not elected, to deal with Britain's greatest crises after World War II. Moreover, Sunak was brown, young as well as relatively inexperienced; only seven years had passed since his first election as an MP and his selection as PM. He is a Hindu and not a Christian, nor a Muslim. The following article on him was written years ago when he had just become Prime Minister of Great Britain.

Rishi Sunak is not the youngest Prime Minister in British history. William Pitt the Younger in the eighteenth century was only twenty-four years old when he was elected to the top job. He brought prosperity to Britain as never before, and ruled continuously for twenty-two years. He died, as it were, in his chair at the age of forty-six. Pitt had planned to generate such a budget that before the end of his rule, the treasury would be so rich that, thereafter, the country could live off the interest earnings so that the people would have to pay no tax. Unfortunately for him and his people, Napoleon Bonaparte, in his expansionist urge to be the master of all of Europe, had declared war and Pitt had to finance it.

Prime Minister Rishi Sunak might find this interesting. Under all these circumstances, he has few alternatives other than finding a magical or miraculous formula to prevent Britain from falling into a financial ditch. However risky the formula, he would have to carry the risk. He happens to have told the Conservative Members of Parliament that they have no other choice but "unite or die". We now ought to tell him that he must "succeed or perish" in public life.

First things first: as an answer to the inflation, in the UK's small but reliable food chains to a small section in every store, the five most basic items of food at fixed reasonable prices ought to be available. If any extra expenditure is to be incurred, the government must step in to pay. Such a measure would ensure that no citizen, however poor, would have to go to bed hungry. No inflationary spiral would then claim lives. A full belly would avert the onslaught of inflation on the populace.

As the first step to obtain the finances needed, a 10 per cent cut on all heads of expenditure would save approximately £100 billion. This would enable immediate action without the fear of going wrong either politically or economically. Apart from dealing with a weak national economy, the next threat would emerge from a global recession and falling exports. Another £100 billion cut must be aimed at. To locate the heads under which this saving can be made, some time to study, think and debate with experts and colleagues would be required. For this, the government must take an entire month of consideration so that there are no blunders of haste.

Thereafter, attention can be devoted to bilateral trade agreements. To start with, an Indo-UK accord would be desirable. The economies of the two countries are comparable in size; plus, the officials and business persons of the two countries should be familiar with each other's ways of working.

For example, we are familiar with the Rolls Royce automobile and engine, and the post-War British combat aircraft, which were the initial mainstay of our air force. We cannot forget that we purchased *INS Vikrant*, our first aircraft carrier, from the Royal Navy. There would be a long list of things we can buy from and export to the UK, from computer chips to spare parts for industrial machinery. Modern Britain was built on the innumerable exports from India. Many other countries would trade with Britain, especially if the British prices were more reasonable to compete in the global market.

Knowing the British character, the Conservative Party would most likely remain united so long as Rishi Sunak appears to be delivering efficiently. The better Sunak performs, the more the opposition Labour Party is likely to get impatient. In any case, this particular opposition party carries the image of being pro-Pakistan. It should also be realised that in the event of failure, Britain's only refuge would be to merge with the USA; say, as four states, England, Scotland, Wales and North Ireland. These four states should be rewarded with eight Senate seats. If Hawai in the Pacific Ocean can be a part of the USA, why cannot there be states of that country in the Atlantic Ocean? After all, Britain after the Second World War has been entirely in the American camp in its foreign policy.

An Oxford veteran, travelling in 1950, in connection with the automobile industry, was so cut up with the loss of the brightest jewel in the crown, vented his disappointment. "My country will now head towards either sinking in the ocean or merging with America".

Medical Education in Other Languages

The move by the National Medical Commission (NMC) to provide medical education in Indian languages is a bright idea. There are any number of students who are competent at studies, although not competent enough to understand and express themselves in English. To exclude them from learning medical science is plainly unfair. Imagine several hundred bright students on the one hand being excluded and on the other, letting quite a few comparatively mediocre youngsters become doctors, simply because they happen to know English. Not only is this grossly unfair, it is also tantamount to denying the country of potentially good doctors. We cannot forget that a preponderant majority of our people are more comfortable speaking and hearing their mother tongues, rather than English. So far, we have insisted upon being treated by doctors who have studied medicine only in English. Do we not see the paradoxes in this system, whose seeds were sown in Sir Jamsetjee Jeejeebhoy Hospital, which founded in its premises the renowned Grant Medical College Mumbai (then Bombay) in the year 1858? The first degree was awarded in 1863, in the style Licentiate of Medicine (L M).

The British had the vision to upgrade this foundational degree to Licentiate of Medicine and Surgery (LM & S) when elementary allopathic surgery was introduced in India. Subsequently, the medical studies were upgraded to MBBS; MD and advanced studies were added in due course. Why should India be left behind and not credit itself with a revolution in the languages of teaching of medicine?

In the tea gardens of northeast India, until recently, the smaller estates employed LM & S; they were generally addressed as "Doctor Babu". The larger estates often employed MBBS-qualified personnel, who would be called "Doctor Sahib". There was no embarrassment at having these two categories in a single community of enterprises. Why then, should there be any objection to a Tamil doctor and an English one, and perhaps a Hindi doctor in Telengana?

Language is not crucial in the study or practice of medicine. There was a surgeon in the Saurashtra region of Gujarat who sailed to London to obtain the degree of Fellow of Royal College of Surgeons (FRCS). He failed for two successive years. He was then advised by an older friend to try Edinburgh, which he did, and passed in his first attempt. It was years later that I discovered the cause of his uneven performance. The FRCS system was such that its examination did not require either a written test or any enquiry in the surgical room. The examiners and the candidate would sit across and discuss for about half an hour or so. This young man could not express himself lucidly in English and thus failed. The Scottish doctors in Edinburgh were perhaps more sympathetic regarding language and expression, and the candidate passed. In the course of the next fifteen years, this candidate became a surgical star. His right hand with the surgeon's knife worked like magic. He operated on almost every part of the body because there was no comparable surgeon in his day.

Rishi Charaka, the father of Ayurveda, mastered the alimentary canal from the lips to the anus, without opening any human body. Some of the medicines invented by him are still considered the best for digestive problems. Charaka's innovation of *rasayana*, the art and craft of rejuvenation needed the patient to stay in a room without sunlight for at least sixty days. He/she had to consume such food and drink that they could clear their bowels scrupulously in the same sixty days. Thereafter, the medicines came into play for another month or so, by which time the patient looked ten to twenty years younger. How much was the role of language in this treatment? Incidentally, about the only language Charaka knew was Sanskrit.

Notwithstanding these circumstances, at some ends of the rural society in India, there are patients without doctors and at other urban ends there are doctors without patients. Why not, therefore, encourage doctors who may not know English?

Sushruta was an ancient Indian physician and surgeon. The *Sushruta Samhita* (Sushruta's Compendium), a treatise ascribed to him is one of the most important surviving ancient treatises on medicine and is considered to be a foundational text of Ayurveda. The treatise addresses all aspects of general medicine, but Sushruta's impressive work on surgery contained in this compendium has led to the erroneous impression that surgery is the sole topic of the *Sushruta Samhita*. These detailed accounts of surgery also have given Sushruta the identity of being the "Father of Surgery". Among the ancient sage's notable contributions to this discipline are his works on early rhinoplasty, classifications of burns into four degrees explaining the effect of heat stroke, frostbite and injuries from lightning, introducing mock surgeries on inanimate objects, a code of ethics for teachers as well as students, classification of eye diseases into seventy-six categories, introduction of wine to dull the pain of surgical incisions and the classification of the types of bone dislocations. None of this seminal work was conceived or written in English. Yet, this ancient Indian sage's work on medicine is accorded the position of being one of the pioneers of surgical medicine.

One Script Rather than One Language

India has chased the shadow of a national language long enough. It is time we thought of a more effective, easier and acceptable alternative. Why not a common script instead? If non-Hindi people feel a clear disadvantage, this has to be removed. A Gujarati would have to learn three languages while the Bihari need not go beyond knowing his own mother tongue plus English. Recommending that everyone should learn three languages, saying the Bihari must know Tamil does not go far. As wishes go, this is a pipedream.

A pragmatic approach should be to follow the practice on highways. A Hindi speaker travelling from Bihar to West Bengal would cease deciphering road names in Bengali. A Tamilian entering Kerala would face the same problem. A common script should overcome this difficulty. Thus far, the English or Roman alphabet has filled the role of a script. Mysteriously, all drivers seem to be able to read signboards and vehicle number plates painted in English. That is why the Centre had stipulated painting number plates of motor vehicles in English letters. To make sure that this instruction was followed, all private car number plates were ordered to be in English letters painted in black on white, while commercial vehicles were to have the numbers in yellow on black. The regional script is disallowed for vehicles.

Kakasaheb Kalelkar, the scholarly freedom fighter, had studied this problem in-depth and concluded that after Independence we should begin with a common script and not a common language. His study concluded that Gujarati letters were the clearest and also did not belong to a majority of speakers and would thus not stoke any resentment against a majority. However, that was over seven decades ago. We could take a fresh view now. Might we zero in on the Roman alphabet? Such an experiment was tried in the army when Hindustani was written/printed in this alphabet for British soldiers to learn the language. British youngsters who came to serve in government or in commerce were taught elementary Hindustani. Incidentally, Gandhi favoured this idea.

Another advantage of the English script would be that children would simultaneously be ready to learn, type and write the English language. It has by now ascended to the position of a universal tongue and is the lingua franca of the Internet. Moreover, the alphabet is not merely English but also serves West European languages; Spanish, French, German, Italian, Polish *et al.* It is only when we reach the Slavic or East European region that the Cyrillic script takes over. Looking ahead in time, there is a possibility that the Chinese and Japanese tongues may one day shift to the Roman alphabet. These Oriental languages do not have a script but only pictographs. Each thought, idea or item is represented by a picture. A Japanese scholar told me that one could make do with knowing five thousand pictographs but a scholar knows up to 50,000. The Chinese alphabet world is said to contain 100,000 pictographs or symbols, though one could get by with knowing between 3,000 to 5,000 of them. One can imagine how easy or difficult this is. Would not thinking be more difficult with pictographs than with alphabets? The mind would have to expend much of its energy remembering pictographs before thinking begins. I feel that maybe one day such languages could shift to the Roman alphabet.

In India, a voluntary beginning with a single script should evoke no resistance; incentives could be offered. If in a school there are five divisions, one of them could teach in the single script and its pupils be charged a distinctly lower fee. No force or compulsion need be brought into play. A great benefit of this experiment of a common alphabet would be that when accepted, a major barrier between Indian languages would disappear. Many of our languages mixed would produce an enormously rich Indian tongue. It would indeed be a great Indian language. The rest of the world would also find it easier to learn it because of its script. The learner would plunge straightaway into the language itself. Indians would come spontaneously closer to one another and also move closer to the rest of the world without even trying!

In all likelihood, this proposition is likely to run into opposition. My Urdu teacher reacted by stressing that the *ruh* or soul of the language would perish. My answer to him was that the Urdu script was about the same as Persian, whereas more Urdu speakers in India are closer to the Arabic world. Yet they have not raised any objection.

Many Bengali, Tamilian and speakers of other languages would protest against this dilution of their respective scripts; justifiably so. However, the richer the language, the greater could be its contribution to the growth of the great Indian language.

Same Sex Marriage

The author has an extended family in Canada. Years ago, their daughter 'married' a girl of Chinese origin. They lived together happily, and still continue to do so. Although, the Chinese partner met a white man at work in her office; they happened to get sexually attracted and produced two children who were brought up in that same sex home. So now, the five of them stay together. Does same-sex marriage, therefore, make any sense?

Marriage is defined as a union whereby men and women are joined in a special kind of social and legal dependence for the purpose of founding and maintaining a family. If it is found that two members of the same gender do not wish to marry in the normal way, but wish to be bound together for life, for succession of property and other rights, there may be another law and another name for the combination. This is necessary so that there is no confusion regarding marriage, which willy-nilly implies founding a family with children.

In Gujarat, there was an institution called *maitree karar* (it probably still exists), which was innovated by a distinguished lawyer Mahendra Vyas. This was meant to accommodate a second lady, who would not be a wife, but would be entitled to inheritance rights. A number of couples in Gujarat have found *maitree karar* useful; no one has confused it with marriage. The children born of such an arrangement are considered legitimate in society, although their position under law remains doubtful.

To highlight a fundamental point, same-sex cohabitation has not been envisaged by nature. Most societies looked upon this idea as a crime against nature. Beyond this belief, same-sex combination is nothing short of legitimising, if not encouraging, homosexuality and further encouraging childlessness. This means further encouraging the depopulation of a society. It is estimated that in the course of a hundred years, there may not be any people left in Japan; its birth rate is not keeping pace with its death rate, although many Japanese live well beyond a hundred. But merely because India has lately experienced an increase in population does not mean that such fecundity is a permanent feature of any civilisation.

The Centre, in this ongoing debate, has opposed any move to accord legal sanction to same-sex marriages in India. Decriminalisation of Section 377 of the Indian Penal Code does not automatically translate into a fundamental right for same-sex couples to marry, the Centre's counsel has said to the Delhi High Court in an affidavit.

The Centre has cited the Supreme Court's earlier ruling, which has granted same-sex couples the freedom to lead a dignified private life, but allows them only "basic right to companionship so long as such companionship is consensual, free from the vice of deceit, force, coercion, and does not result in the violation of fundamental rights of others".

The world over, a large body of growing scientific and sociological evidence points to the fact that an intact, naturally married family is best for the upbringing of children. Only a biological family can ensure that children have access to the time and money of two adults, the mother and father. And only a proper family can provide a system of checks and balances that makes quality parenting possible. The indispensability of the biological connection to the child that both parents can provide increases the likelihood that the parents would identify with the child and be willing to sacrifice for that child. Homosexual couples, on the other hand, can only create a situation where their supposed children will have to miss either a mother or father.

If same-sex civil marriages become common, most same-sex couples with children would be lesbian couples. This would mean that we would have yet more children being raised apart from fathers. Among other things, it has been found that fathers excel in reducing antisocial behaviour and delinquency in boys and sexual activity in girls.

Under the pretext of modernisation, with new legislation like legalising homosexuality, let us not jettison the natural joy of producing and raising children and then hoping they would grow up and help take care of parents in the their old age. This has been the pattern for centuries, especially in Asian societies. A visit to Europe would enable one to meet many single parents as well as their children. In the bigger cities of the continent I have been to, I have been told that only about 20 per cent of the people marry conventionally. The rest live together and occasionally produce children. In the event of a separation, children normally go with the mother. Several mothers in Germany have said that their children were irresponsible and non-committal towards society. The point is that we need to think a lot more on various aspects of life, collective as well as individually, before legislating on same-sex marriage. We should not imitate the West, since conditions in Asia are very different.

Hinduism

It is interesting to see that many Westerners of stature are taking keen interest in Hinduism and have lately called it a scientific religion. Whoever conceived and authored the Vedas must have given enormous thought before explaining the Sanatan Dharma, a faith that does not lean on the concept of God. If anything, it relies on the individual choosing his own *dharma* and then attempting to fulfil the challenges thus laid down. This is rather like an explorer choosing his destination and proceeding to reach it. How far he reaches is his own business. He may proceed straight and fulfil his *dharma*, or fall a little short, or perhaps very short. Or, as often happens, he might stray from his path of *karma* and eventually be reborn as a much inferior being. The best he can achieve is not to be reborn, achieve *mukti* (liberation) or salvation as the Christians would call it.

This is the core of Sanatan Dharma. In terms of logic, it resembles the path of Inductive Logic. This branch of reasoning, or *logos*, as the ancient Greeks would call it, expects every action to evoke a reaction, equal and opposite. Curiously, this is similar to one of the foundational principles of physics, which might have induced scholars to have called Hinduism scientific. Inductive Logic begins with the gathering of data on the ground and begins reasoning upwards to a conclusion.

Deductive Logic is the other segment of the discipline of logic. The deductive approach is quicker and crisper, because one does not have to travel through the labyrinth of reasoning, for there is no conclusion to arrive at. Deductive reasoning begins with a given premise, which is presumed to need no authentication.

Take Judaism, founded by Prophet Moses, who in his Ten Commandments, ordained from Mount Sinai that our only God is Jehovah and there is no other god. What he or his prophet ordained is Judaic truth. This then is the supreme premise accepted by every Jew. Its chain of corollaries that follow is the substance of Judaism. Because the corollary or corollaries have emerged from the premise, there is little scope for dispute or dissidence. The Judaic faith has over the centuries shrunk no doubt, but has not split.

In sharp contrast, one can say that in Hinduism there are as many denominations and religious orders as there are temples and places of worship. In that context, Hinduism is a riot of democracy and yet, it is a shining example of Inductive Logic in action. There are few societies or civilisations that have been invaded by Islamic conquerors, and have not turned Muslim. Not only India, which is a Hindu-majority country, but the subcontinent too has retained its Hindu majority. The Sanatana freedom has been its greatest strength; not only in terms of followers, but also in terms of scriptures. Hinduism has thousands of historic places of pilgrimage in India alone. The number of scriptures in the religion is innumerable.

Non-violence, aversion to killing and preference for

vegetarian food should be traced to an abiding faith in the transmigration of the soul at the end of death, except until *mukti* is attained. The apprehension of a Hindu is that any living being he meets might be carrying the soul of someone who might have been a near and dear one in a previous life. The sympathetic attitude to vegetation or any other aspect of ecology is again attributed to the fear of killing insects and other living beings. This is particularly emphasised in Jain theology. Be it a Hindu or a Jain, the comparative emphasis is on the soul as distinct from the body. In fact, the mortal frame is considered an object of pollution after death; not to be preserved, but cremated as soon as possible.

It is appropriate to stress that the single greatest strength of Hinduism is its demand for action in terms of *karma*. Several other religions depend on the followers' belief, or the worshipper's faith in the word of the prophet or priest that there is only one god, that there will be a doomsday or *Qaiamat* and on that occasion, God will decide whether an individual will be sent to heaven or hell. Until then, the individual's body will remain buried.

This is an enormous challenge to the worshipper's credulousness. In contrast, Hinduism expects the follower to choose his or her own *dharma* or duty and perform *karma* in his or her endeavour to live up to *dharma*. There is no challenge or compulsion to believe, or imposition upon the adherent's intelligence. It is freedom all the way.

Having outlined Hinduism in terms of inductive logic, it is only fair to conceptualise as to what would happen as an effect of a religion that is aligned to, or an outcome of Deductive Logic. The Abrahamic faiths are classic examples of such religions. Each one of them asserts that their god is the only god and only under his auspices can one reach heaven. The first corollary is that every altruistic follower must endeavour to bring as many humans as possible under the umbrella of his god. The next corollary would be twofold; one, to give birth to more children and increase the number of members of the religion. Second, converting those outside the fold of the religion into believers is a quick way of increasing the followers of one's religion. Incidentally, allowing and encouraging polygamy is a part of the religions outlook of these religious, as is the prohibition of celibacy and encouragement for the use of aphrodisiacs.

Not encouraging education, especially of women, is an important aspect of variants of Deductive thought. An uneducated woman is unlikely to appreciate the value of studies for her children. The less educated a parent is, the less questioning he or she would be about the laws and rules prevailing, unless changes are considered desirable by the clergy.

The result of these corollaries makes the societies emerging from those ideologies or belief systems power-oriented, which in turn, produces a mentality and mindset of dominance. "What we think and say is right, and if you do not agree, a conflict will result," is the credo of this outlook.

At home in India, we witnessed unprovoked invasions through 712 AD to 1761 AD (when the Third Battle of Panipat was fought). In the meanwhile, invasions by sea had already begun, and another set of foreigners ruled till 1947. This total period of foreign rule exceeds twelve centuries. The story, however, does not end here.

On August 14, 1947, the world of Abraham again had its say; it cut India into three, the two wings of Pakistan and the remaining Bharat. Not even twenty-five years had passed when the two wings of Pakistan fell apart. Since 2023, the western wing of Pakistan has been reduced to beggary.

The partition of the country has reduced West Pakistan to unthinkable poverty, while the eastern wing has had to borrow money on a large scale. One may turn from Asia to Europe, whose history has been an endless catalogue of war after war. The biggest two wars, the World Wars, ensured the decline of the European continent; and yet, no historian has been able to justify why on earth were these wars fought.

Take the European war of 2023 between Russia and Ukraine, which were until 1991, virtually inseparable partners of the world's largest country geographically. Nothing can explain this war except the itch of Deductive Logic, leading to an irrepressible ego.

On Ayodhya

After centuries of foreign domination, Hindus from all walks of life, whether rich or poor, high or low, asserted for the first time that Rama, the seventh avatar of Vishnu and his birthplace belongs to us (i.e., the Hindus). Allama Iqbal, the famous poet called Rama the "Imam-e-Hind". Other Muslims also have conceded that he was an avatar of a Hindu divinity. When, however, it came to handing over his place of birth, the consistent reply was a resounding "no". On the other hand Hindus solemnly believe that Rama's birthplace was not only in the city of Ayodhya but also at the spot where Mir Baqi, a general of Babar, the Timurid invader, built a large edifice. What a shame that the invaders sat on Rama's birthplace after burying the temple with that enormous three-dome structure! Incidentally, this construction did not have a single minaret, which was so necessary for the muezzin climbing up to call people for prayers, five times a day. Perhaps four minarets to a mosque may be built for the sake of symmetry but certainly a minimum of one is essential. In Anatolia, Turkey, most mosques in the rural areas have only one minaret.

Another essential for a masjid is a *wuzoo*, as one enters the building to enable the worshipper to wash his forearms as well as feet. The edifice at Ayodhya did not have one. All this made one feel that the structure at Ayodhya was intended to be a *dargah* or mausoleum, possibly for Babar himself, when one was needed eventually. When the Sunni Muslims took over the defence of the edifice from the Shias, they began calling it a mosque, the Babri Masjid. Their perception could have been that in the event of the Hindus demanding *Ram Janmabhoomi*, it would be easier to resist and save a mosque rather than a *dargah*. In the former, God and prayers may be involved, whereas in the latter, a mausoleum is only a memorial. It is difficult to think of a mosque named after a conqueror and this is one more reason to believe that Babri Masjid was a contrived name. It takes a long time to demolish a structure or to build one. Babar lived for only four years after his conquest in India. How long did his general Mir Baqi last in India? It couldn't have been for many years. Agreed, that these are details of conjecture. Nevertheless, they are relevant. Babar, of course, was mostly busy fighting with Rana Sanga in 1527 and Medini Rai of Gwalior later that year. The consolidation of his conquest must also have consumed a lot of his time and energy. Nor could Mir Baqi have been free to solely be preoccupied with Ayodhya.

The point being made here is that to bring down the Ram Lalla temple and to erect a huge edifice comprising ten thick walls with a spacious *chabutara* adorned by three enormous domes, all of which had long durability must have taken some time.

Incidentally, nobody had been informed of what precisely was going to happen on December 6, 1992, except that extensions were going to be made to the earlier *shilanyas*. I had accompanied the future chief ministers of Gujarat; Messrs Keshubhai Patel and Sureshchandra Mehta. We were all placed on a VIP terrace, which was supposedly on the *Sita ki Rasoi*. We had ascended it by 10:40 am, but could not go down or come up again before 5:30 pm. We had fasted with no food or water all day until we reached Lucknow that night. Unfortunately, dinner was delayed, because somewhere along the journey, Keshubhai's attaché case containing some 4,000 rupees was stolen; this was discovered only after we reached our rooms in the guest house.

Between 11 and 12 noon, a number of young men had climbed on to the domes which was presumed as a grave threat to the safety of the domes. I learnt about this threat from the foreign correspondents whom I met many days after the event. They told me that these urchins enticed them into bringing out their cameras to photograph them. Their attention then was drawn to take snaps of the muscular men who were systematically striking at the edifice with crowbars. The blows were being aimed at the intersection of the dome with walls below them. The photographers were asked by the hefty men not to take any photographs. When the press personnel did not pay heed, a few of the workers came out of the edifice, across the *chabutara*, presumably to prevent the press people from clicking any photographs. The police intervened in the nick of time, and quickly whisked away the five correspondents into a nearby temple, and locked them up in a small room. They were not allowed to come out, except to be given their meals. The journalists were released only after 5pm in the evening, and taken to their hotel in Faizabad. To return to the terrace, the only mike available was being handled by Acharya Dharmendra, to engage and entertain the vast crowd that had gathered below. Any other speaker who wished to use the mike was allowed to do so.

At about 1:30 pm, two press photographers rushed up to the terrace. Their faces were bleeding as they had been manhandled by the men who did not wish to be photographed. Evidently, the men were employed in an organisation that would not tolerate their personnel getting involved in an activity like the *kar seva*. When their earnest requests were not heeded by the press photographers, they snatched the latter's cameras and smashed them, also pulling out their film rolls to destroy them. They suspected that the *karsevaks* might have been government employees. They were using crowbars to try and separate the domes from the walls. This would be sufficient to cause the domes to crash. A lady IPS police officer spoke to me and clarified that the police had instructions to intervene only if there was a real danger to anyone's life. Otherwise, the government wanted the police to keep off. The photographers' lives were not in any danger; it was they who were obstinate in wanting to click photographs. At 2:30 pm, the first dome nearest to the Saryu River collapsed. After that young men in groups carrying stones or marble pieces were visible. They were carrying these away as souvenirs. One particular piece, I can recall, was long enough to require eight boys to carry it. Archarya Dharmendra became more animated than before and so did most people on the terrace. The middle dome did not fall until 3:40 pm. The souvenir collection picked up further pace. Finally, the third dome went down at 4:30 pm.

The giant domes that had dominated the Ayodhya skyline for 450 years were now nothing more than *Surkhil* (red brick powder) mingled with sand. When we left Ayodhya a little after 5:30 pm, it was very cold and pitch dark. But one could still figure out the shadows of the structure's walls standing securely, like torsos without heads. By the crack of dawn on December 9, (60 hours later) where the structure stood was plain ground, except for a small portion occupied by a small tent, from where Ram Lalla's icon, as though surveying all of Hindudom, rested. The tent, guarded by the Central Reserve Police was surrounded by many coins, totaling about Rs. 9,000, mostly signifying the devotion that the police and security personnel felt for Lord Ram.

Until December 6, 1992, Indian history does not record any event wherein Hindu hands adversely touched a Muslim shrine. That makes the demolition of the edifice at Ayodhya an iconic event, whereby Hindus joined together to demolish a 450-year-old enormous edifice. No doubt, there were Hindu leaders who suffered trepidation as to what would follow. Mostly out of fear of retaliation, and some out of pangs of conscience euphemistically called secularism.

One leader, who at one time had led the Ayodhya movement, said in a written statement that the December 6 event was the "darkest day in my life". However, no one is on record to say that it was as significant a turn in India's history as the defeat and death of Prithviraj Chauhan in the Second Battle of Tarain in 1192, and again, on August 14, 1947, when India was partitioned. That makes December 6, 1992, the third most important turning point of Indian history. Since 1192, for nearly a millennium, temple after temple was desecrated with Hindus weeping and wailing helplessly. Since 1947, the Islamic load on Hindu shoulders was much reduced; 1992 released forces that enabled Hindus to begin coming into their own.

Jinnah, His Persona

Without Mohammad Ali Jinnah, most likely, there would not have been a partition in August 1947. The Muslims of the subcontinent had not thrown up a leader of any calibre who could argue, persuade or compel the departing British rulers to grant a separate Pakistan. The Muslim League members had realised this in time and with the help of Nawabzada Liaqat Ali Khan induced Jinnah to return to India in 1935 from his much-preferred cozy home in Hampstead, London.

The Muslim-majority provinces, namely, Bengal, Punjab, NWFP (the North West Frontier Province), Sind and possibly Baluchistan, would have been the regions to combine and become Pakistan. As it happened, they already had premiers who were Muslim, members of the legislative assemblies with Muslim majorities, who ruled these Muslim provinces. Where was then the need for them to separate from the rest of India? In fact, by separating, they ran the risk of losing the then national market. The Muslims, in the provinces where they were in a minority, needed the comfort of an Islamic entity like a Muslim homeland, but they could get this only by migrating to Pakistan.

This meant being uprooted from their familiar environment and adjusting to an alien one. Their own provinces could not transfer to Pakistan. Clearly, a partition of India did not make sense.

The challenge before Qaid-e-Azam Jinnah was to make sense out of non-sense. At the same time, to carry the Muslims of India with him on this quest of his, he had to approach the British rulers and convince them that they would gain by the creation of Pakistan. The general British thinking at the time was that to keep India on their side would be easier, whereas two Indias was likely to mean that one of the two could go the opposite way. The Hindus, then led by the Congress were against the division of their country, or *Bharatmata* in any way being imputed. Hardly any Muslim looked at his community in a mirror from the economic perspective. The region, they could claim for Pakistan were largely devoid of industry. Even his elite in the heartland was land- or orchard-owning; possessing neither much industry nor business. Only the Gujarati Muslims, namely the Bohras, Memons and Khojas were endowed with any business experience, which was inherited from their Hindu origins. Jinnah had neither the leisure nor the education and nor in fact, the interest to understand the economic capabilities of the world-be Pakistanis. His obsession was with founding a new country and thus cock a snook at Mohandas Gandhi. The former's exposure to politics until 1915 was debate and discussions in paneled chambers of lawyers and others. He detested street politics and was at sea when he had to deal with it. Jinnah spoke only English with the fluency required in making speeches. He could converse in Gujarati, but that was about all. He could not address his audience in Gujarati during public meetings, even while electioneering. One can imagine how Herculean his task must have been. When he finally failed to complete or even coexist with Gandhi, Jinnah left the Congress for good and decided to settle in London. He was on the verge of bidding goodbye to politics as well.

Into his legal practice in the UK, whose environs and social life he loved so dearly, Jinnah built a reputation of being the highest paid barrister in the British Empire. He returned to India only on the condition that he would be forthwith elected as the life president of the Muslim League. When the League could not perform particularly well in the 1937 provincial elections held in India, Jinnah brought forth his now famous Pakistan Resolution of the party at the Lahore session of his party on March 23, 1940. Just the previous day, in a long speech, he explained to his partymen and community, the logic for his demand for a separate state of Pakistan. In all probability, Jinnah might have said to himself that if Gandhi denied him the space to effectively achieve a position of leadership in the Congress, he would show the Mahatma his place by partitioning his country.

Jinnah had a younger brother, Ahmed Ali, who was a good friend of my grandfather Dharamdas Vora. He would often visit my grandfather's home at Girgaum, Bombay in the afternoon, where the two friends would chat away till evening. In the course of one of their afternoon chats, the younger Jinnah told my grandfather that his older brother simply had to be number one in anything he did. He had now found his avenue to attain his cherished goal of reaching the hall of fame in history by carving out a place as the founder of a new country. He had little other consideration that would stop him from racing to his goal or wondering whether his Muslim compatriots were competent or equipped to run a nation. In fact, his knowledge or familiarity with them was, for a leader, non-existent. As his brother Ahmed Ali revealed to my grandfather, they (the

Jinnahs) were culturally more Parsi than anything else. His elder brother Mohammad married a Parsi lady of an affluent and elite Bombay family; the lady's name was Ruttie. His only child, Dina, also married a Parsi, Neville Wadia.

The ancestry of Mohammad Ali Jinnah is even more interesting. His paternal grandfather was Premji Meghji Thakkar, belonging to the Halai Lohana sub-caste, who are strict vegetarians. Thakkar was a trader based in Dhoraji about 70 kilometres, from Rajkot and Porbundar. At some stage, Premji Thakkar's traditional business suffered a decline. His well-wisher, a Khoja Muslim, suggested that Premji try his hand at trading in fish. The advice proved sound economically, but the caste leaders of Premji's community strongly disapproved of anything non-vegetarian. A time came when the leaders asked him to choose between either his business or his caste. Premji did not have an economic option and thus suffered expulsion. He then took refuge in becoming an Ismaili Khoja.

Premji's son was Poonja, who continued with the business as well as being a Khoja. Poonjabhai, in turn, begot Mohammad Ali. The family had used their ancestor's name Jina meaning tiny, for generations, and called themselves "Jinabhai". In the course of his four-year stay in London, Mohammad Ali excluded the suffix 'bhai' from his name, whereby he became Mr M A Jinnah. He showed no attachment to any religion, for he neither prayed, nor did he abstain from consuming alcohol and pork sandwiches. According to brother Ahmed, they did not even have the attire required to perform *namaz*, until Jinnah became the life president of the Muslim League. By then, he had transformed himself from an Ismaili Khoja to an Asna Ashri Khoja, so that his being "full Muslim" could not be challenged by any politician.

There was a particular reason for this intra-sect conversion. In 1861, a division bench of the Bombay High Court had declared the Ismaili Khoja sect to be "half-Hindu and half-Muslim" because their inheritance laws were the same as those of Hindus. No wonder, Jinnah was the arch example of a secular politician until he was driven to "teach Mohandas Gandhi the lesson of a lifetime" and at the same time unwittingly, vastly reducing the Muslim load on Hindu heads. Sometimes, one wonders whether that was a subconscious throwback to his Thakkar genes. In any case, it was an ironical equation for two men, both barristers, both hailing from the Saurashtra region of the state's Peninsula. Porbunder and Dhoraji, the respective native places of Gandhi and Jinnah, are separated by a mere 70 kilometres.

To go back to the effort the Qaid-e-Azam Jinnah had to undertake in order to make Muslims vote in favour of Pakistan, he began with his own members. His argument was that Muslims were fewer in numbers than the Hindus, who were more educated. The latter also dominated trade and industry. If the governments were to be elected by adult franchise, the policies of the Congress would have a greater say and its professed leanings towards socialism would nationalise the *zamindaris* and *jagirdaris*, which would seriously damage the interests of the Muslims. The departure of the British from India would thus place Islam in danger. Those last three words were Jinnah's campaign slogan.

When the elections of 1945-46 came around, Jinnah used this card to drum up support. He succeeded in generating a political whirlwind in favour of Pakistan, which he portrayed as the 'New Medina'. In the provinces where Muslims were in much smaller numbers, they responded vociferously to the magic of Jinnah. They really needed a separate country because of their numbers, although their provinces could not go to Pakistan geographically. Some prepared to migrate, although these were comparatively few in number. Nevertheless, they experienced an unusual feeling of satisfaction and voted for it. They did not care for the fact that their New Medina had, come into shape in the strangest way, with its constituents separated by more than a thousand miles, which was the approximate distance between the two wings of Pakistan, East and West.

Be that as it may, nearly two-thirds of the Muslim load was taken off Hindus by Partition. Imagine, what would have been India's situation, if there had been no vivisection. And there would have been no Partition had there been no Jinnah, with his irrepressible ambition to find a place in history's hall of fame. Having achieved his Pakistan, the Qaid-e-Azam did not live long; say, a mere thirteen months. About half of this period of time was spent by him resting in Jiarat, some distance from Quetta in Baluchistan. When his health began failing, he was flown back to Karachi, where he died late in the evening of the day of his arrival. He was buried the next day in all glory, including his attire, which was not the sherwani and *pyjama*, but his favourite Saville Row suit.

Happiness

When happiness is discussed it is taken for granted that it is a single concept and for those who experience it, it is the same emotion. A large number of people are influenced by their religion to weigh their experiences on the scale of their faith. Broadly, those who lean on religion should be divided into at least two segments. One would be the Abrahamics, i.e., Jews, Christians and Muslims; the other segment comprises of Hindus, or adherents of those faiths that have emerged out of Hinduism, like for example, Jainism. Yet another section would be those who are substantially disconnected from religion, and lead a life on what they believe to be secular premises.

Happiness often gets mixed up with other emotions, such as satisfaction. Like, someone might say that he/she is happy with the work he/she does. Someone else might feel that he experiences happiness when he scores a century in a game of cricket. Both satisfaction and bliss are ephemeral emotions; they are not happiness. Happiness is a much more ongoing emotion, a feeling of ongoing fulfilment rather than pleasure, or delight, but certainly not satisfaction, which is a strong but generally a fleeting emotion of one or two desires.

One example of happiness that comes to mind is a professor of economics, who rose to be the principal of Mumbai's prestigious Sydenham College of Commerce. His one great passion was to teach, and the better his students performed, he said the happier he was. Apart from imparting his knowledge, he had nothing to give his students, who in turn gave him respect and affection. Many of them called on him at least once a year for decades to come. He passed away 29 years after he retired, and yet nearly all his former students attended his funeral.

To a believing Hindu, a spiritual experience, even if only once in a lifetime is an exhilarating memory and an inexhaustible source of happiness. The example that comes to mind is that of Swami Vivekananda. His spiritual master and mentor Swami Ramakrishna Paramahansa once enabled him to have a direct *darshan* of the divine. Sri Aurobindo in his Puducherry ashram had a similar experience, which his disciples believed filled his life with fulfilment.

The Abrahamic religions, especially Judaism and Islam, do not encourage such spiritual adventures. In fact, their religions expressly forbid any conceptualisation or visualisation of the divine form, image or idol. Prophet Moses explicitly laid down in the third of his famed Ten Commandments: "Thee shall not make any gravel image of thy lord the god". But the adherents of the Abrahamic faiths have the facility of their scriptures which guide them in detail about what all to do and avoid. There is seldom a need to have to think or solve questions of day to day life. However, when a member of the Abrahamic family of religions does occasionally experience happiness, with its potential highs, it is a happening than needs to be investigated.

Their readiness to get involved in wars, quarrels, disputes

and skirmishes is well-known. At the time of writing, there are two unprovoked wars, one in Ukraine in Europe and the other in Gaza in the Middle East still raging.

A Hindu has the facility of accepting his lot in life, because he believes that that is what he deserves in the light of his *karma* in the past, both distant and recent. This includes previous births and lives as well. In fact, *karma* is the core of Hindu belief, which he performs in the context of his chosen *dharma*. He is free to choose what the *dharma* or mission in his life is, or ought to be. If he cannot choose, he can rely on his caste to guide him.

The Hindu, therefore, does not have to rely on his ambition to measure his success or failure, whereas the Abrahamic religion follower may aspire for the sky; he may or may not reach it, and remain on land to his utter disappointment. The atheist and the agnostic also has no guidance whatever, except what they think and perform in their current life.

Frustration stems from the lack of assessing either one's ability or the adequacy of one's effort. Desire, however, is no justification for or equation to any fulfilment. Of course, there are other emotions that lead to unhappiness. An outstanding one is jealously, suffered by many an individual. Another weakness is the propensity to anger, which is, almost, temporary insanity. Greed again is yet another weakness that tempts people to do things that are not feasible. These three emotions are evidently enemies of happiness. While completely uprooting them is impossible, the human being, in his or her own interest, should make every possible effort to eschew them or rise above them.

National Council for Education and Research

News is that the National Council for Education and Research (NCERT) is likely to recommend the teaching of the Ramayana and Mahabharata to students of Classes VI to XII in schools. This is indeed news to be welcomed. However, the proposal for the epics to be taught as part of classical history is less than desirable. India's two great and timeless works are epics, which magnetically draw their readers and portray classical Indian culture in two mighty sweeps. The Ramayana is a classical portrayal of idealism, while the Mahabharata paints a mega picture of realism. One tells the reader what life should be while the epic of Veda Vyasa is an immortal work. Possibly all the shades human nature can exhibit with or without provocation are contained in the Mahabharata. The classical age of India and its culture is portrayed between the two mega epics.

Having stated all this in praise of the two great epics, it must be said that neither is a work of history, which is the selection of facts about the past that are relevant to the future. Admittedly, no civilisation other than Indian has the privilege of having produced anything comparable. Nevertheless, both works are examples of mythology rather than history. Whether Maharshi Valmiki or Veda Vyasa gave a free play to their imagination as much as their knowledge—as they contemporaneously witnessed what happened—is not in question. Had it been, these epics would not have been so electrifyingly absorbing, whether to an illiterate commoner or to an intellectual whose mind has been developed in a university. Some would say that minds are dulled in universities, an opinion that is difficult to dismiss.

The Oxford Dictionary defines history as "a continuous, typically chronological record of past events or trends". The same lexicon defines mythology as "a set of widely held, but exaggerated or fictitious stories or beliefs". In this context, it would be useful to know that the historicity of Shri Krishna has been corroborated by Prof Shobha Mukerji of Lucknow University in her book *The Republican Trends in Ancient India*. Shri Ramachandra is certain to have been a real figure, but no historian as yet has underwritten his historicity.

However, it must be admitted that history as a discipline was not recognised or even realised until the nineteenth century. Sir Jadunath Sarkar, the most distinguished Indian historian, in fact, belonged to the twentieth century. The ancient Indian authors were more mythologists than historians, while the recorders of the medieval Islamic period were nothing more than chroniclers. The only major Indian work reputed to be in the realm of history was the *Rajatarangini* by the Kashmiri scholar Kalhana, written sometime during the eleventh or twelfth centuries.

But we are discussing the NCERT's proposal to include the Ramayana and Mahabharata as part of the school syllabus for the coming generations. From a school student's point of view, whether he is reading a work of history or mythology is not important, so long as he or she realises the difference. It is vital that students know the glory of the civilisation and heritage they are born into and belong to. Right or wrong, one generally sees a firm view or conviction when it comes to other civilisations or religions. Most of the Islamic rulers believed that whatever existed before the period of Hijri (the Islamic calendar, i.e., the advent of Islam) was *jahiliya* or an era of darkness. British rulers began by believing that European civilisation was supreme. Until they discovered the marvels of Hindu civilisation and culture, they carried on in their beliefs of European superiority, and also actively implemented the same in the course of their rule over the subcontinent spanning nearly two centuries.

For the Indian student however, organised printing and publishing began at Serampore, a suburb of Calcutta. A British priest was the foremost initiator. For decades, most of the literature printed and available for sale was in the English language and, therefore, of British origin. Change did take place; however, the expediting cause was the ideology of Karl Marx; in other words, the fundamental inspiration was Communist. One of the very important channels of communicating Marxist propaganda was through printed material, mostly books. Many educated persons have their fundaments sown in Marxist thought. The centrists and right wingers, until recently, had little conception of how modern educated Indians were influenced by socialist thinking. It is overdue that Indian students are awakened to the richness of their own past. For this particular purpose, there is nothing more apt than to begin with the Ramayana and the Mahabharata. The Bhagavad Gita, in simple translations should also be published separately.

As part of the Mahabharata, the significance of the Bhagavad Gita may be missed by a youngster. The simplified translations of the two epics have been produced excellently by Chakravarti Rajagopalachari, the first Indian Governor-General after Independence.

By introducing a new course called mythology, other aspects of Indian literature can also be brought in such as the Vedas, Upanishads, Puranas, the various Simritis and so on. Today, few Indian young men and women are aware of these monumental contributions of their country to world civilisation.

School for Political Education

There are in India about six lakh legislators including all the panchayats. The Parliament plus all the state assemblies have nearly 5,000 members, plus the lady members, following the legislation for women's reservation in elected bodies. But hardly a few of them have any educational exposure to management or theories relating to the subject. It is not their fault for two good reasons; one, they are normal citizens who happen to get elected and not because they are qualified to either legislate or to execute the laws. Second, except for a rare few, they do not get the opportunity to be exposed to any management studies. There is not a single school for national governance.

A fundamental truth, that politics is the engine of society, has been overlooked. Many a vocation, including hair-cutting, leather work *et al*, have organised facilities for training, not to speak of the various management schools. To practice his vocation, the politician has no organised facility to equip him to become a more effective leader. Strangely, this is not merely an Indian oversight, but a general one. Other countries too suffer from this lacuna. In India at least there is no organised facility to tell the political worker that politics is for serving society primarily, whereas the personal enjoyment of prominence and power are only secondary perquisites.

Governments in India have promoted management schools, some of them quite effective and of global standards. In the early days after Independence, the only such professional institution was one at Hyderabad called the Administrative Staff College, which was run effectively. It was a government-promoted institution. Many young men and women aspire to be political leaders and would be ready to pay for professional training, provided it is affordable.

The first subject that should be taught is communication from the platform, particularly on how to speak, but also what to eschew while communicating from public forums. Three aspects need to be borne in mind. One, there are veterans who can hold audiences of about fifty thousand to a lakh of people in their constituencies, spellbound, but become dumb if asked to communicate in a legislative house. I knew a veteran from Ahmedabad, who had also served as the leader of Opposition in the state assembly. He had been elected to the Lok Sabha too, and had been an MP for ten years. In all these years, this gentleman did not speak even once; in fact, he did not ask a single question inside the house. There was another member who represented the Amreli Constituency, also for ten years, who opened his mouth only once. That was when his question happened to be starred. This gentleman's question was about the fishermen on the Gujarat coast. As was the rule, the MP got two chances to ask supplementary questions to a minister's reply on the floor of the house. In Gujarat, the same gentleman was a popular public speaker, but inside Parliament, he did not speak either before or after his supplementary questions, in all his ten years of life as an MP. Why? The answer is that neither of these two MPs were fluent in Hindi. They could deliver speeches in Gujarati in the house, provided they gave a week's notice, so that an interpreter could be specially arranged by the Secretariat.

But a speech needs to be prepared and perhaps practised. Why take so much trouble when the people who sent these political representatives to Parliament lived far away in their respective constituencies? By impressing the house, they weren't going to be made ministers. Some newcomers, especially to the Rajya Sabha, had to read out their speeches, as they could not speak extempore. In my time as a Rajya Sabha MP, such a practice was strictly not allowed and a special case had to be made for the maiden speech.

In course of time, more and more of such members must have entered Parliament. Every legislator should have a working knowledge of how the Constitution of India was drafted, and its essential contents, including the important amendments. Minus this knowledge, especially in Parliament, issues under discussion go over the head of several members, especially MLAs, who could miss out on the rights of states. To add to this working knowledge, members must also be aware of how the States' Reorganisation Commission redrew the map of British India and what happened thereafter. This information could be useful also for panchayat members.

Thirdly, knowing basic facts about our country is essential for those wishing to play a public role. Aspirants should know about the media *per se*, particularly its functioning in India, and also the factors that motivate media barons and working journalists, plus the differences between the magazines, dailies and the electronic and digital media.

Fourth, a working knowledge of the independence

movement in the twentieth century, the Partition, and its consequences on the three constituents of the subcontinent, must be the essential knowledge for anyone aspiring for political office. Fifth, knowledge of the Indian economy, its society and sociology including castes and various reservations is necessary. Sixth, an analysis of the history of the subcontinent must be included. There are several other subjects essential for every political aspirant to know.

How Cricket Came About

As an adult pastime, the beginning of cricket is remembered as being around four centuries ago. In style, schedules and spirit, it did not change much during this time. Nevertheless, it has grown so much as to have become the number two sport in the world in terms of popularity, next only to football. This is despite most of its players, clubs and teams hail only from the erstwhile British Empire.

Remarkably, cricket had customs that would be unthinkable today. Players until the early twentieth century were 'gentlemen', some also aristocrats. The Indian captain of those days was always a maharaja, until Vijay Merchant led the team in 1946, midway during that year's cricketing season when the then captain, Nawab Iftikhar Ali Pataudi, fell ill in England. English captains were strictly gentlemen, who did not live off any aspect of cricket, their names printed with initials and never the first name.

The inclusion of professionals also brought separate gates for them in the pavilions, distinct from the gates for gentlemen. Professionals' names would be printed as their first names like John, Richard or Mortimer. They dared not use either their initials or the gentlemen's pavilion gate. The English captain was always a gentleman until Len Hutton was made captain in 1952.

Change was slow in the game of cricket. The One Day International (ODI) might not have taken off but for the revolutionary intervention by Kerry Packer, who commercialised cricket on a scale unimagined hitherto. Packer's experiment ended in three years, but he introduced the ODI, day and night cricket and coloured cricket arguably forever.

Then, in later years came the T20 or T#20 game, enabling viewers to enjoy cricket for the same duration as a movie. A great deal changed, including the colour of the ball. There were no noticeable changes in the strategy of bowling. For example, in a Test Match, the principal aim of the bowler is to take wickets. Bowlers received applause for the wickets they bagged in an innings and the match. In an ODI, the bowler aims to concede as few runs as possible in a match. However, watching the matches played these days, one gets the feeling that most bowlers are hungry for wickets and are less bothered about the runs scored off their balls. Sixes and fours are hit galore. Hundreds of them were clobbered during the World Cup 2023. Bowlers were applauded whenever they took a wicket but seldom admonished for giving a couple of sixes in an over. I felt pained whenever an Indian bowler gave away a six or a boundary and would retreat into the comforting memory of Bapu Nadkarni who played for India in the 1960s.

He was a spinner but could bat at No. 7 or 8. In a five-day Test match, the batsmen could afford to score runs at ease. Nadkarni gave away very few runs, although he took fewer wickets. His best bowling analysis that I know of was 30 overs, 27 maidens, 7 runs and no wickets.

Such bowling in an ODI would be a dream. With pressure building on the batting side, no batsman can tolerate Nadkarni's style of bowling; good-length delivery after good-length delivery, never conceding a short ball. I don't think Bapu ever bowled a full-toss in any match. In an ODI or even T20, such bowling would harass the batsman to the point of insanity, forcing him to play a shot to get out. Only in an occasional match did Nadkarni bowl fast; all six balls in the over were yorkers.

In an ODI, the bowler's primary task is not to take wickets but block runs and force batsmen to get out by losing patience. Batsmen's patience will run out if they are prevented from scoring. One ODI provides batters only 300 balls to score a winning total. The least the bowler can do is to ensure that none of his 60 balls (ten overs) rise to the level of the batsman's knee; deliveries must be kept at that length or below.

Traditionally, bowlers have been described as the attack but in a one-day match it is the batsmen who don that role, as they have to make runs as quickly as possible. Anything outside the leg-stump is a wide-ball; effectively, a no-ball. Shouldn't the batsman, therefore, take guard outside the off-stump? Most balls would come on between the middle and off-stump, or outside. Batsmen can hit towards the leg side where generally there aren't many fielders. In trying to force shots to the leg-side, batsmen are likely to offer more catches on that side. For ordinary batsmen, legside shots are much easier than offside ones.

Vijay Merchant, Vijay Hazare and Russi Modi used to play most of their strokes on the offside rather than leg. They were class batsmen. I wonder what the great Ranjitsinhji would have done had he gotten to play ODIs. I am curios because Ranji was an inventor of strokes. It was he who brought in aggressive scoring shots behind the wickets in England, especially the pull, glance and sweep. Until his time, except for the occasional cut, most behind-the-wicket shots were incidental and not by design. This was Ranji's greatest claim to fame.

Hindu Values can Save Humanity

At the recently concluded World Hindu Congress in Bangkok, Thailand's Prime Minister Srettha Thavisin unequivocally declared that Hindu values alone can bring about peace in the world. In the light of the many conflicts that are currently raging in the world, Mr Thavisin's endorsement does merit examination.

It is no secret that Hinduism values the life of all beings, even inanimate objects. Transmigration of souls or rather the faith in its journey is the primary cause of the Hindus' preference for nonviolence to deal with issues or solve problems. Admittedly, there are violent Hindus, but comparatively few. The subconscious apprehension in the average Hindu's mind is that there might reside the soul of his long-deceased relation or forefather in the body of an adversary who he might inadvertently make a victim. The possible victim might also be an animal or bird. Vegetarianism is a corollary of the belief in transmigration.

The Indian vegetarian accepts milk and milk products readily, whereas the Western vegan does not, because milk is the property of the mother of a calf, which has all the right to consume it. An upright Hindu's reluctance to cut a tree, more so a peepul or banyan tree is the fear complex about whether vegetation has life or not. In the belief and conduct of the Jains, aversion to killing even an insect is an extension of the same aforesaid aversion to violence. Lord Buddha had a clear preference for the vegetarian way of life.

The Hindu individual's aversion to bloodshed logically extended to society and even beyond, to all humanity. Notably, only four major Hindu figures resisted foreign invasions against India in the second millennium; namely, Rana Sanga, Maharana Pratap, Raja Hemachandra aka Hemu and Chhatrapati Shivaji. There are fewer other notable revolts against foreign invaders on record.

This does demonstrate the Hindu aversion to taking a life. In sharp contrast, the history of Europe is virtually a catalogue of war and bloodshed. Take the history of only the twentieth century; WWI, often referred to as the Great War, began with the murder of the crown prince of the Austro-Hungarian Empire, Archduke Franz Ferdinand, by a Serb vagabond. Was there no other way of punishing the assassin than take the lives of 17 million people in the course of four years?

Napoleon Bonaparte is one of the most glorified figures of European history. Yet, what did his many battles achieve, other than leaving France as no longer the premier European power, apart from the innumerable soldiers who perished on the many battlefields? World War II followed a mere twenty-one years after WWI, as a vengeful consequence of the Great War. Large tracts of Europe were bombed into debris apart from sixty million people perishing. What did such a grievous sacrifice achieve? Nothing, except the decline of Europe. And yet, the Continent has not learnt its lesson. At the time of writing, Russia has invaded its own previous republic, Ukraine, nearly four years ago, at a cost of over two hundred thousand human lives.

Two other faiths of the Abrahamic family are currently fighting it out in the region called Palestine. Prophet Abraham was the father of Western religions, who began life in Mesopotamia. Thereafter, when he codified religion, he moved to Canaan, or where Israel is currently situated. Out of genuine belief, as well as for the sake of unity, Abraham declared that there was only one God. Seven hundred years later, Prophet Moses confirmed that there was only one God. Fourteen hundred years later, Prophet Mohammad repeated the same sentiments, when he exhorted women to love their husbands and bear children, so that a day might come when his devotees outnumber those of any other community.

Since then, Christianity and Islam have converted more and more pagans and *kafirs* into their own respective faiths. The religious texts of the three Abrahamic faiths contain sections that support violence and justify warfare as a means to achieve certain goals. In particular circumstances, these texts have served as the basis to legitimate violent campaigns, often against communities of other faiths. Many of the passages from religious texts in all three religious traditions are used in contemporary situations to support violence and war, whether interpreted literally or misinterpreted.

The moment these faiths—all of which were born in West Asia—changed from being 'faiths' to 'religions', they became politically charged, and discord became inevitable at that point. In an era when the average person couldn't read or write, they would go to religious services and someone would read holy books to them. The clergy, which was literate compared to the flock of followers, soon realised they could tell people just about anything and claim it was the word of the Almighty. Briefly, this is how religions are born out of faiths. While faiths are beliefs, religions are institutions that historically have a political agenda.

Viewed in the light of the current world scenario, the Thai Prime Minister's reminder is more than timely.